The Vegan Cookbook

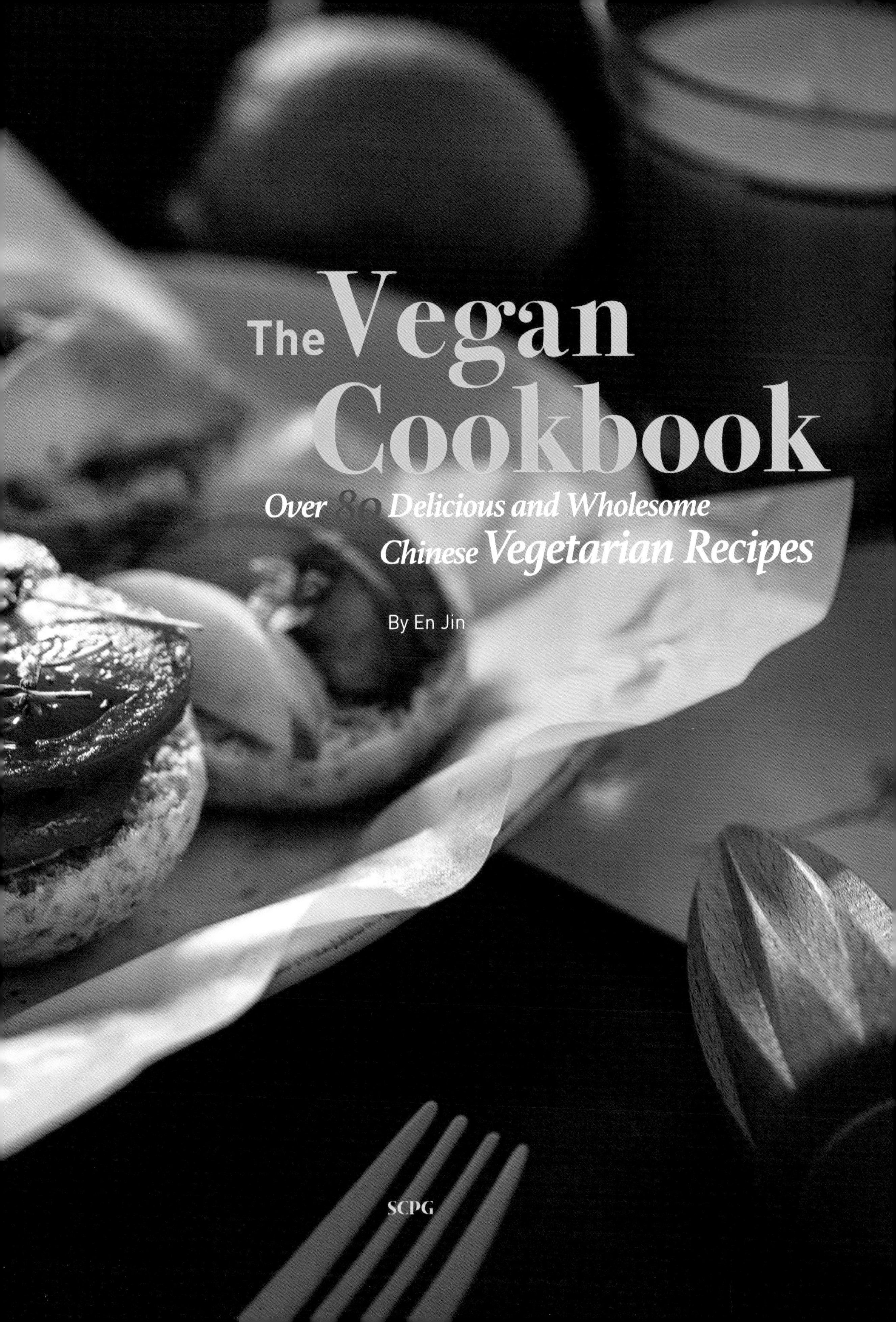

The Vegan Cookbook

Over 80 Delicious and Wholesome Chinese Vegetarian Recipes

By En Jin

SCPG

Text and Photos: En Jin

Translation: Shelly Bryant
Cover Design: Shi Hanlin
Interior Design: Hu Bin, Li Jing (Yuan Yinchang Design Studio)

Editor: Cao Yue
Assistant Editor: Yang Wenjing

ISBN: 978-1-63288-024-6

Address any comments about *The Vegan Cookbook: Over 80 Delicious and Wholesome Chinese Vegetarian Recipes* to:

SCPG
401 Broadway, Ste. 1000
New York, NY 10013
USA

or

Shanghai Press and Publishing Development Co., Ltd.
Floor 5, No. 390 Fuzhou Road, Shanghai, China (200001)
Email: sppd@sppdbook.com

Printed in China by Shanghai Donnelley Printing Co., Ltd.

1   3   5   7   9   10   8   6   4   2

Contents

Preface   *7*

Chapter One   Introduction of Whole Plant-Based Diet   *11*

Chapter Two   Whole Grains   *27*

Chapter Three   Legumes and Seeds   *45*

Chapter Four   Root Vegetables   *81*

Chapter Five   Green Leafy Vegetables   *123*

Chapter Six   Fresh Fruits   *151*

Chapter Seven   Mushrooms   *191*

Appendix   Conversions   *208*

Preface

*T*he *Vegan Cookbook* is my second book. When I received the commission from the publishing house, the editor informed me that the readers of this recipe book come from all over the world. So I thought about how to share my cooking experience and food philosophy on vegan cuisine with readers from different cultural backgrounds.

China boasts a long history and has many indigenous and unique ingredients, as well as distinctive cooking methods. I am eager to introduce more locally sourced Chinese ingredients to readers and transform these ingredients into plant-based dishes. For me, these ingredients are not only rich in nutritional value but are also filled with long-lasting historical accumulation and deep cultural meaning.

I have been practicing a whole plant-based diet for over six years. My dietary philosophy involves consuming only fresh vegetables, fruits, legumes, grains, nuts, seeds, and completely abstaining from dairy, eggs, meat, and honey.

In this book, all the recipes I share are dishes I have experimented with in my daily practice, following the principle of balanced nutrition and featuring Chinese-flavored plant-based cuisine. I believe they can provide everyone with a unique and pure experience of whole plant-based eating.

Some of the fresh vegetables and fruits I use come from my own countryside vegetable garden. Throughout the changing seasons of spring, summer, autumn, and winter, from sowing to harvesting, to washing and cooking, I take my time and carefully prepare each ingredient that I've grown and enjoy the tranquility that this process brings me.

Another portion of the ingredients comes from chance discoveries in the countryside across various regions of China. Through this process, I have had the pleasure of meeting interesting individuals such as farmers and advocates of natural farming methods. Experiencing the joy of discovering wild vegetables and fruits in the mountains and fields has brought me much healing and inspiration. It has also allowed me to appreciate how natural ingredients from the wilderness can nourish both body and soul. I feel that life is good when I can share healthy and natural food with like-minded friends. I feel uplifted by these mundane daily experiences. I am grateful for the food granted by the mountains and fields, allowing me to do what I love and live the beautiful life I envision.

This book will take you into the mountains, forests, and fields, delving deep to explore unique and abundant ingredients, and the relationship among ingredients, nature, and the body. In the first section, I will introduce some of the distinctive wild ingredients found in China, as well as commonly used cooking tools and seasonings. In the second section, the ingredients will be divided into six categories, whole grains, legumes and seeds, root vegetables, green leafy vegetables, fresh fruits, and mushrooms. Using these ingredients as a guide, I will incorporate traditional Chinese seasoning and cooking methods to create over 80 fusion plant-based dishes blending Eastern and Western influences, including main dishes, snacks, desserts, and more. The complexity of the recipes varies, but I have provided detailed preparation steps for each one. I believe that by following along with me attentively, even kitchen novices can easily create these delicious and healthy plant-based dishes.

The recipes in the book, such as the whole plant-based bowl featuring leafy greens and fresh fruits, can be adapted by substituting with seasonal local ingredients. Quantities of ingredients can also be adjusted according to preferences to create personal delicious dishes. I hope this book will inspire you in the kitchen and bring you joy through cooking.

Chapter One
Introduction of Whole Plant-Based Diet

In recent years, whole plant-based diet has become a popular new vegetarian lifestyle embraced by an increasing number of people worldwide. It involves consuming only fresh vegetables, fruits, legumes, grains, nuts, and seeds. This dietary lifestyle is not only environmentally friendly and kind towards animals but also beneficial for both our physical and mental health.

Plant-based ingredients grow naturally and absorb abundant energy from nature, possessing strong vitality. Roots, stems, leaves, fruits, and seeds of various plants are rich in a variety of nutrients. By diversifying and scientifically combining these ingredients and adopting minimally processed cooking methods that preserve the original flavors of the food, it is entirely possible to meet the daily nutritional needs of the human body.

Fig. 1 Ingredient database.

Establishing an Ingredient Database

To better follow the recipes in this book, it is recommended to establish an ingredient database first.

As a practitioner of whole plant-based eating, the most important aspect of cooking is adhering to the principle of balanced nutrition and diversifying the food to ensure the daily nutritional needs of the body. Having a well-stocked ingredient database increases the flexibility of ingredient combinations while minimizing the time spent searching for ingredients. This lays a solid foundation for subsequent cooking endeavors.

My ingredient database is generally divided into two categories, dry ingredients and fresh ingredients. Dry ingredients are convenient for long-term storage, while fresh ingredients follow local seasonal plant-based foods. In this book, recipes are created based on ingredients, which are categorized into six main groups, whole grains, legumes and seeds, root vegetables, leafy greens, fresh fruits, and mushrooms. The majority of whole grains, legumes and seeds, and mushrooms belong to the dry ingredient category, while the rest fall under the fresh ingredient category.

To store dry ingredients, package them in airtight containers, label them with expiry dates, and store them in a dedicated pantry or cabinet. Cultivate a habit of regularly organizing and rotating stock. It is advisable to stock up on a quarter or half year's supply at a time.

For fresh ingredients, prioritize purchasing naturally grown or organic produce whenever possible. Purchase fresh ingredients locally and choose according to seasonal availability. If it is feasible, consider establishing a small herb garden for fresh spices, such as basil, rosemary, mint, and edible flowers, on a balcony or in a small space to ensure a steady supply of fresh spices.

Chinese-Origin Ingredients

Some of the ingredients used in this book originate from China with a long history. During the process of creating this book, I visited various mountains and fields to explore each ingredient. There are extraordinary stories behind the ingredients. The fragrant food made from these ingredients warms the stomach and soothes weary nerves, nourishing depleted souls.

Brown Rice (糙米 cāo mǐ)

The cultivation of rice originated in China, and it is also a staple food in Chinese households. The commonly used rice in the recipes of this book is brown rice. Brown rice is rice that has undergone coarse processing, whereas further processing turns it into white rice. Brown rice requires more water to cook thoroughly, allowing for better digestion and absorption by the body.

---

* You may find the Chinese ingredients at those websites: *www.sayweee.com* and *www.freshgogo.com*.

Soybeans (大豆 dà dòu)

Soybeans are cultivated worldwide, but they have a history of cultivation in China for over five thousand years. They are seeds rich in plant protein. Soybean-derived products such as tofu and tempeh hold significant importance in the vegetarian community.

Red Beans (红豆 hóng dòu)

Red beans are commonly used kitchen ingredients with medicinal properties. They are suitable for stewing soups, cooking porridge, or making desserts.

Black Beans (黑豆 hēi dòu)

Black beans have a cultivation history of over four thousand years. They are rich in protein, various amino acids, and fats, making them a nutritious ingredient.

Water Shield (莼菜 chún cài)

Water shield, one of the "three famous vegetables of Jiangnan (an area in China to the south of the lower reaches of the Yangtze River)" in China, is exceptionally tender, smooth, and crispy, representing a unique aquatic wild vegetable in southern China.

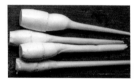

Water Bamboo (茭白 jiāo bái)

Water bamboo, a perennial aquatic plant, is consumed for its fleshy stem. It is white and tender, the flesh is glutinous and soft. Braising it with soy sauce or dry-frying it results in a very tender texture and fresh taste.

Lotus Root (莲藕 lián ǒu)

Lotus root is slightly sweet and crispy, suitable for raw consumption or cooking. Some lotus roots have a crunchy and tender texture, ideal for stir-frying, while others are starchier and more suitable for stewing.

Water Chestnut (荸荠 bí qí)

When eaten raw, water chestnut is sweet and juicy. It can also be used for making soup or tea. With versatile culinary uses, it effectively clears heat and relieves internal fire in the body.

Arrowhead (茨菇 cí gū)

The arrowhead originates from southeastern China. It has a soft and glutinous texture, tender in flesh, slightly bitter in taste, but with a sweet aftertaste that lingers in the mouth.

Shephard's Purse (荠菜 jì cài)

Shepherd's purse is a popular wild vegetable which is often hailed as the king of wild vegetables. It is nutritionally rich and highly valued for its medicinal properties. It also lends a delicious flavor to dishes when cooked with various ingredients.

Chinese Toon (香椿 xiāng chūn)

Chinese toons are tender buds that grow on Chinese toon trees in spring. Their sprouts are highly nutritious and seasonal, with a fresh and unique flavor. They can be used in various ways such as in salads, pancakes, and steamed rice, offering a wide range of cooking possibilities.

Red Amaranth (红苋菜 hóng xiàn cài)

Red amaranth is produced abundantly in the summer, and has been consumed as a wild vegetable since ancient times. Its leaves are soft and smooth with a strong vegetable flavor, and are often used in soups or stir-fries. It is known for its ability to nourish the stomach and clear heat from the body.

Purple Perilla (紫苏 zǐ sū)

Purple perilla is native to China, and is often added to various dishes to enhance their flavor profile. It is also a versatile ingredient with medicinal properties.

Persimmon (柿子 shì zi)

Persimmon is truly representative of the Chinese taste, originating from the Yangtze River basin in China. There are nearly a hundred varieties of persimmons, and they can be prepared in various ways. Dried persimmons, persimmon sauce, and persimmon desserts all offer delicious flavors.

Mandarin Orange (柑橘 gān jú)

China is the original center of citrus fruit trees in the world, boasting a wide variety of excellent varieties with over four thousand years of cultivation history. Various citrus fruits are frequently used in this book, not only for their rich nutritional content and sweet-and-sour taste but also for the strong citrus aroma they lend to dishes.

Pear (梨 lí)

China has a rich variety of pear species, with widespread cultivation. Late summer to early autumn is the prime season for consuming pears, as they are moisturizing, lung-nourishing, and nutritious.

Peach (桃 táo)

Peaches hold significant importance in Chinese culture. Not only are they delicious, but they also carry positive symbolism, representing wealth and longevity. Peaches are low-calorie, high-fiber fruit rich in natural antioxidants.

Hawthorn (山楂 shān zhā)

Hawthorn is native to China, but as a fruit, it is too sour for most people to eat directly. When made into hawthorn cakes or hawthorn pies, with some maple syrup added for flavoring, it becomes sweet and sour, appetizing, and refreshing.

Lily Bulb (百合 bǎi hé)

As a traditional Chinese medicine, lily bulbs nourish *yin*, moisten the lungs, calm the heart, and soothes the nerves. As a food, they are suitable for stir-frying or making porridge, offering a crisp and mildly sweet taste.

Lychee (荔枝 lì zhī)

Lychee is native to southern China, with its cultivation and consumption history dating back to the Han dynasty (206 BC–AD 220). One of the most famous stories associated with lychee is about Yang Guifei (719–756), one of the four great beauties of ancient China, who loved eating lychee. Lychees are harvested in summer, and when chilled, they become cool, refreshing, and deliciously sweet, making them a delightful treat on hot summer days.

Monkey Head Mushroom (猴头菇 hóu tóu gū)

Monkey head mushroom is one of the eight great "mountain delicacies" in China. It is tender and flavorful, delicious, and a valuable traditional Chinese medicinal ingredient with functions that aid digestion and benefit the five organs.

Oyster Mushroom (平菇 píng gū)

Oyster mushroom is one of the most common mushroom varieties in China. They have smooth, thick caps, with a smooth, tender, and slightly crisp texture.

Chestnut (栗子 lì zi)

Chestnuts have a long history of cultivation in China. In ancient times, Chinese chestnuts were considered a precious food, often used in banquets and important occasions. Today, due to their soft, sweet taste, chestnuts have become a popular snack loved by many.

Yam (山药 shān yào)
Yam originates from Shanxi Province in North China. When stir-fried, it is crisp and refreshing. When stewed, it becomes soft and tender. Its sticky juice helps maintain vascular elasticity, moistens the lungs to relieve coughs, and provides excellent protection for the digestive system.

Bamboo Shoot (竹笋 zhú sǔn)
Bamboo shoots are a distinctive taste memory unique to the people of Jiangnan. Throughout history, Chinese gourmands have considered bamboo shoots to be the finest of vegetarian dishes. Fresh and crisp, bamboo shoots represent the taste of spring.

Fish Mint (鱼腥草 yú xīng cǎo)
Fish mint (Houttuynia cordata) is primarily distributed in southern China and has a unique flavor. In addition to being used as food, it has significant medicinal value, including clearing heat and detoxifying, diuretic and anti-swelling effects, and antibacterial and anti-inflammatory properties.

Waxberry (杨梅 yáng méi)
Waxberry is a quintessential Chinese fruit with a cultivation history of over two thousand years. It has a tart and sweet flavor profile. Besides being eaten raw, waxberries can also be used to make waxberry soup, waxberry ice jelly, dried waxberries, canned waxberries, and more.

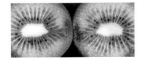

Kiwi (猕猴桃 mí hóu táo)
Long ago, kiwi was a wild fruit growing on trees. It has a sweet and refreshing taste, with soft and juicy flesh, and is rich in vitamins.

Daylily (黄花菜 huáng huā cài)
Daylilies originated in northeastern China and are one of the eight great "mountain delicacies." They are fresh and tender, low in calories, and rich in various nutrients such as vitamins and amino acids.

Mugwort (艾草 ài cǎo)
Mugwort is a widely distributed medicinal plant with a long history of use and consumption in China. During the Dragon Boat Festival, it is customary to hang mugwort on the door. When added to food, mugwort imparts a fragrant aroma and a fresh taste, and it has medicinal properties that warm meridians for dispelling cold.

Common Cooking Utensils

The commonly used cooking utensils in this book's recipes are relatively simple. I will divide them into three categories, cookware, kitchen appliances, and practical kitchen tools. These utensils are common items, so before cooking, review the utensils in your kitchen. If you already have something that can serve the same purpose, there's no need to purchase duplicates.

1. Cookware

Wok

A wok is a basic piece of kitchen equipment. Chinese-style woks typically have a longer diameter and deeper inner diameter, making them convenient for stir-frying. They are commonly used for stir-frying vegetables or cooking dishes with sauces. Woks come in various materials, but I typically use a non-stick wok. Not only is it easy to clean, but it also requires less oil, resulting in healthier and cleaner dishes.

Frying Pan

The frying pan is perhaps my favorite piece of cookware due to its versatility and ease of use. It has a wide range of applications. The frying pan is shallower than a wok, but if there aren't many ingredients, it can also be used as a substitute for a wok. I also often use it as a baking tray, heating it up, and then turning to low heat. It's very convenient for toasting bread in the morning. It can also be used to fry vegetables. Brush some oil on the bottom of the pan, spread out mushrooms, asparagus, and other vegetables, and cook them over low heat. I often use this method to make plant-based bowls. The frying pan is also perfect for making plain pancakes and various vegetable pancakes. In short, if you don't have small appliances like ovens or air fryers, the frying pan is a very practical alternative.

Small Soup Pot

The small soup pot is also a commonly used utensil in the kitchen. It is suitable for cooking vegetable broth, various stews, or quickly blanching vegetables. It's also very convenient for cooking single-serving noodles because you can serve them directly from the pot without transferring to a plate. If you need to fry food, a small soup pot with a slightly deeper inner diameter is also safer.

2. Kitchen Appliances

Food Processor/Hand Blender

Food processors are commonly used to chop ingredients and make sauces or thick soups, whether you need to grind

Fig. 2   Food processor (left) and hand blender (right).

ingredients into a fine powder or puree, a food processor can do it quickly. Hand blenders are often used for quickly making sauces because they are easy to clean and eliminate the hassle of transferring ingredients to a food processor. That's why I use them frequently as well.

Fig. 3   High-speed blender.

High-Speed Blender
High-speed blenders are widely available on the market with various brands and powerful capabilities. People can choose them according to their needs. If you're using it alone, purchasing a smaller-capacity blender is sufficient. High-speed blenders are essential tools for practitioners of a plant-based diet. I use mine almost every day, primarily for making various plant-based milks rich in plant proteins and smoothies packed with dietary fiber and vitamins.

Rice Cooker
Rice cookers are commonly used to cook grains like brown rice. Choose a rice cooker with a whole grain function, which can more accurately control the texture of the grains.

Toaster Oven
Toaster ovens are commonly used for baking or reheating foods such as bread, pizza, cakes, sweet potatoes, broccoli, and more. Making breakfast or brunch with a toaster oven is not only convenient but also eliminates the hassle of dealing with smoke from frying.

3. Practical Kitchen Tools

Vegetable Spinner
The vegetable spinner is something I use almost every day. It's commonly used for drying salad greens, fruits, and other ingredients used for raw consumption. If you enjoy eating salads, it's definitely a must-have tool.

Measuring Spoons
Measuring spoons allow for quick and precise measurement of seasoning ingredients. I've been using the ones from IKEA. There are many options available on the market, so I recommend choosing ones that are durable, easy to clean, and easy to store.

Fig. 4   Measuring spoons.

Fig. 5   Digital scale.

Fig. 6   Manual juicer.

Digital Scale

A digital scale provides a precise measurement of various ingredients through specific numerical values, making it a very useful tool for cooking novices who haven't developed a sense for ingredient measurements yet.

Manual Juicer

I often use lemon juice, orange juice, or grapefruit juice to create sauces with different flavors every day. However, since the quantities needed are usually small, this manual juicer is particularly practical. It helps avoid waste and is easy to clean.

Common Seasonings

The seasonings used in this cookbook are relatively simple. I believe in using the simplest cooking methods to highlight the natural flavors of food with good ingredients. Here are some of the common seasonings used in this book.

Vegetable Oil

There are numerous brands of cooking oil available on the market. When I shop, I follow the principle of buying small bottles and diversifying my choices. I try to avoid purchasing large bottles of cooking oil and instead opt for small bottles with the freshest expiration dates. Some of the vegetable oils I most commonly use include olive oil, canola oil, sesame oil, and coconut oil.

Olive oil is the oil I use most frequently. It contains abundant monounsaturated fatty acids and various vitamins, making it suitable for stir-frying and cold dishes.

Canola oil is often used for stir-frying and frying. It has the lowest saturated fatty acid content among all oils, making it a good substitute for oils high in saturated fat and thus reducing the risk of cardiovascular disease.

Sesame oil, whether used in noodles or to dress sauces, can be considered the finishing touch, as its rich sesame aroma adds a lot of flavors to Chinese-style dishes.

Coconut oil is commonly used in making desserts and sweet treats. Its delightful aroma blends perfectly with desserts, adding a rich coconut flavor.

Soy Sauce

Soy sauce originated in China, with records of its production dating back over three thousand years ago. Soy sauce is primarily made from defatted soybeans and wheat. After fermentation, it becomes a flavorful condiment. Adding soy sauce to dishes not only enhances their color and aroma but also enriches their taste, achieving a perfect balance of color, aroma, and taste.

Based on the production process, soy sauce can be divided into different types. The ones I often use are light soy sauce (*sheng chou*, 生抽) and dark soy sauce (*lao chou*, 老抽). Light soy sauce has a lighter color and a delicious taste with a rich aroma of fermented soybeans. It is commonly used for seasoning in cold dishes or stir-frying to enhance the flavor. Dark soy sauce, on the other hand, has a darker color and a saltier, richer taste. Its primary purpose is to add color to dishes.

Vegetarian Oyster Sauce

Vegetarian oyster sauce is mainly made from mushrooms. As a seasoning, it is best to choose one without preservatives, added colorings, and with low salt content. It not only offers a fresh mushroom aroma but also provides a savory and sweet sauce flavor. Vegetarian oyster sauce is a healthy and delicious condiment which is commonly used to enhance the flavor of many Chinese cooking methods.

▲ Balsamic vinegar

▲ Vegetable oil

▼ Light soy sauce

▲ Dark soy sauce

▼ White vinegar

Salt

Salt is one of the most commonly used seasonings, and there are many types available. From a health perspective, it is advisable to choose low-sodium salt that contains iodine and minerals. Alternatively, you can rotate between using sea salt, rock salt, and other unrefined salts according to different dishes.

Sugar

Coconut flower sugar is a natural sweetener extracted from the sap of coconut flowers. It hasn't undergone extensive processing, retaining more nutrients and minerals compared to refined white sugar. It has a similar taste to brown sugar, with a high sweetness and a slight caramel flavor. Using it as a substitute for regular sugar is a great choice.

Maple syrup is low in calories, high in calcium, completely natural, and rich in various nutrients. It also has a relatively low glycemic index. I often use maple syrup instead of honey to make sauces and add flavor to various dishes.

Vinegar

Grains have been used to ferment vinegar in China since ancient times. Adding vinegar while cooking not only enhances acidity but also adds fragrance and sweetness, resulting in a unique flavor. I often add vinegar to noodles or cold dishes to stimulate the taste buds and improve the texture.

The raw material for mature vinegar is sorghum, resulting in a darker color and a richer, more intense sour taste. It is typically used in dishes where a pronounced sour flavor is desired.

Rice vinegar is made from rice. It has a light color and a moderately sweet and sour taste, suitable for most people's palates. It is commonly used in cooking green leafy vegetables and can also be used directly in cold dishes.

Black rice vinegar is made from glutinous rice. It is not particularly sour and has a smooth and delicate taste. Because it is made from glutinous rice, it has a hint of sweetness from the starch. It is commonly used as a dipping sauce.

Besides these commonly used Chinese vinegar, I also frequently use brown rice vinegar and apple cider vinegar. Brown rice vinegar has a richer flavor, while apple cider vinegar has a fruity and refreshing taste.

Brown rice vinegar is made from unpolished brown rice, which retains its fiber and amino acids because it is not polished. It can promote gastrointestinal motility, aid digestion, and enhance appetite. It also contains abundant mineral elements, which can improve pancreatic function, enhance sugar tolerance, and control blood sugar levels when consumed.

Another sour ingredient I frequently use is lemon. Lemon contains natural antioxidants and can be used instead of vinegar by adding it to sauces.

Common Homemade Sauces

Next, I will introduce several sauce and broth recipes. Once made, they will greatly enhance the versatility of vegan cooking. Sauces and broths can elevate the flavors of plant-based dishes and are key to enhancing their taste profile.

Plant-Based Cheese Sauce

Ingredients

- 2 oz raw cashews
- 2 Tbsp plant-based milk
- 1 tsp lemon juice
- ¼ oz garlic
- 1 Tbsp nutritional yeast powder
- ¼ tsp salt
- a pinch of black pepper

Instructions

❶ Soak the cashews in hot water for 30 minutes, then drain and pat them dry.

❷ Put the soaked cashews and other ingredients into a food processor and blend until smooth and creamy.

❸ Transfer the prepared plant-based cheese sauce into a sealed glass jar and refrigerate. Consume it within one week for optimal taste and texture.

Tips

Soaking the cashews makes them softer and easier to blend. Soak them overnight, or if it's summer, soak them in room temperature water and refrigerate overnight.

The plant-based cheese sauce can be refrigerated for up to 2 weeks. If you make a large batch, you can portion some and freeze it. It is recommended to consume it within a month.

Peanut Sesame Sauce

Ingredients

- 1 Tbsp peanut butter
- 1 Tbsp plant-based cheese sauce
- 1 Tbsp olive oil
- 1 tsp apple cider vinegar

Instructions

In a small bowl, combine the peanut butter, plant-based cheese sauce, olive oil, and apple cider vinegar. Mix thoroughly using a hand blender.

Sesame Cheese Sauce

Ingredients

- 1 Tbsp pure sesame paste
- 1 Tbsp plant-based cheese sauce
- 1 Tbsp olive oil
- 1 tsp maple syrup

Instructions

In a small bowl, combine the pure sesame paste, plant-based cheese sauce, olive oil, and maple syrup. Mix thoroughly using a hand blender.

Vinaigrette

Ingredients

- 2 Tbsp olive oil
- 1 tsp balsamic vinegar
- 1 Tbsp maple syrup
- a pinch of black pepper

Instructions

Combine all ingredients in a small bowl and mix well. Adjust the amount of black pepper according to personal taste.

Kombu Broth

Ingredients

- ½ oz dried kelp (kombu)
- 1 qt water

Instructions

Rinse the dried kelp (kombu) and soak it in water overnight. Then, simmer over medium heat for about 20 minutes. Remove the kelp and strain the broth.

Pure Vegetable Broth

Ingredients

- 1 oz cherry tomatoes
- 1 oz carrot
- 1 oz onion
- 1 slice ginger
- 1 qt water

Instructions

Wash all the vegetables, add them to clean water, simmer over medium heat for about 20 minutes, strain out the vegetable residue, and retain the broth.

Chapter Two
Whole Grains

The method of pairing ingredients in a plant-based bowl is an inspiration that emerged during my practice of whole plant-based diets. Following the principle of diversified intake, a variety of foods are placed in one bowl, ensuring comprehensive nutrition and rich colors. It is visually appealing and adds pleasure to the dining experience. It divides a meal's dietary structure into four equal parts, or you can think of it as dividing a circular plate or bowl into four equal sections, ¼ carbohydrates (mainly whole grains), ¼ protein (mainly legumes, tofu, tempeh, seeds, etc.), and ½ local seasonal vegetables and fruits.

This chapter mainly introduces the essential component of the plant-based bowl, which is whole grains. Whole grains are grains that have not undergone refined processing or, if processed by milling, grinding, flaking, etc., still retain the intact bran, germ, and endosperm along with their natural nutritional components. Compared to refined grains, whole grains not only provide ample energy for the body but also better retain nutrients such as dietary fiber, B vitamins, minerals, and phytonutrients, which contribute to enhancing immunity and strengthening the body.

Whole grains serve as the foundation of plant-based bowls, and their combinations are flexible and diverse. In this chapter, we have selected several representative whole grains and paired them with different cooking methods to provide you with some inspiration and reference for your plant-based bowls.

Brown Rice with Avocado

Tip

You can replace the vegetables in this recipe with any vegetables you like.

The cultivation of rice originated in Hunan Province, in central China, with a history dating back to approximately 12,000 to 16,000 years BC, so rice is essential on the Chinese table. In a whole plant-based diet, I advocate for the consumption of brown rice. It retains the complete nutrition of rice while offering more fiber and vitamins. You'll love its chewy texture!

Ingredients

A

- 2 oz tricolor brown rice
- ½ oz plant-based protein crumbles
- 2 slices of fresh red lentil
- 2 tsp vegetable oil
- 1 Tbsp soy sauce
- moderate amount of kale

B

- ½ avocado
- 1 tsp seaweed seasoning
- 1 walnut
- 2 slices of apple

Instructions

❶ For set A, soak the tricolor brown rice for 4 to 8 hours. Add water 1 cm above the level of the rice, then boil the rice in a pot for about 20 minutes until done or cook it with a rice cooker using its brown rice setting. Wash the kale thoroughly, shake off excess water, and cut into thin shreds. Drain the water from the plant-based protein crumbles after soaking. Wash the red lentil, and cut into thin slices. Heat vegetable oil in a frying pan, then add the plant-based protein crumbles, shredded red lentils, and shredded kale in sequence, stir-fry until cooked. Add a bowl of cooked brown rice to the pan, and before serving, add a little soy sauce and transfer to a serving dish.

❷ For set B, halve the avocado, sprinkle some seaweed seasoning on top, then add a walnut kernel and slices of apple. Assemble all the ingredients and serve.

Seaweed Brown Rice Rolls Veggie Bowl

This recipe is healthy and rich in taste and texture, and is suitable for packing in a lunch box for a picnic or as a workday meal. As the main item of this dish, the seaweed brown rice rolls will boost energy levels as well as provide plenty of plant protein and dietary fiber with the tofu and celery wrapped within. The accompanying fried tofu is charred and crispy on the outside, yet soft and delicate on the inside, and the sweet and sour black plums perfectly balance the greasiness, making this a refreshing and delicious offering.

Ingredients

A

- 1 sheet of seaweed
- 1½ oz brown rice
- ½ oz tricolor quinoa
- 1 tsp sushi vinegar
- 3 small pieces of tofu
- dash of celery

B

- 1 block of firm tofu
- ½ oz whole wheat flour
- ¼ oz bread crumbs
- ½ c frying oil

C

- ¼ oz frisee
- ½ Tbsp peanut sesame sauce (see page 23 for recipe)
- 1 black plum
- dash of red onions

Instructions

❶ For set A, rinse the quinoa and brown rice, and soak the brown rice for 4 to 8 hours. Add water 1 cm above the level of the rice, then boil the quinoa in a pot for about 15 minutes and the rice for 20 minutes until done, or cook them with a rice cooker using its brown rice setting. Once cooked, allow both to cool before adding sushi vinegar, then mix well. Roll up the rice, tofu, and celery with the sheet of seaweed and cut into half.

❷ For set B, slice the firm tofu and drain excess water, add water to the whole wheat flour to make a batter, dip the tofu slices in the batter, then coat them with the bread crumbs, and deep-fry until both sides turn golden brown.

❸ For set C, rinse the frisee and shake them dry, cut the red onions into thin strips, and drizzle with the peanut sesame sauce. Slice the black plum.

❹ Assemble all the ingredients and serve.

Tips

Chickpeas can be soaked overnight and then rinsed and cooked the next morning. In hot weather, they should be refrigerated after cooking.

Similar legume ingredients can be soaked and cooked in larger quantities at once. After cooking, the remaining legumes can be stored in the freezer compartment of the refrigerator and used anytime.

Rainbow Veggie Salad Rice Bowl

This recipe is my bold attempt to blend Chinese flavors into Western-style salad. The warm brown rice paired with the special almond miso sauce creates a soulful combination with the nutty aroma of the nuts and the unique fermented fragrance of miso, making it fresh, fragrant, and mellow.

Ingredients

A

- 1 oz tricolor brown rice
- ½ oz cooked chickpeas
- 1 oz walnuts
- ½ oz pea tips
- 1 small carrot
- 2 round slices of red radish
- dash of sesame
- dash of pumpkin seeds

B

- 2 tsp sesame
- 4 tsp almond flour
- 2 tsp chopped spring onions
- 2 tsp soy sauce
- 2 tsp aged vinegar
- 1 tsp miso paste
- 2 tsp sesame oil
- 1 tsp minced garlic

Instructions

❶ For set A, soak the tricolor brown rice for 4 to 8 hours. Add water 1 cm above the level of the rice, then boil the rice in a pot for about 20 minutes until done or cook it with a rice cooker using its brown rice setting. Slice the carrot and red radishes into thin shreds. Toast the walnuts in the oven at 100 ℃ for 5 minutes. Blanch the pea tips in boiling water.

❷ For set B, prepare the almond miso sauce. Combine all the ingredients in a bowl and mix well.

❸ Combine the cooked tricolor brown rice with all the ingredients, then add the almond miso sauce and mix well.

Naked Oat Noodles with Tempeh and Tomato

Naked oat is one of the original oat varieties in China. It has the highest protein content among cereal crops. In the western regions of China, people often use naked oat to make a variety of staple foods, which are both filling and nutritious. My favorite is naked oat noodles in the shape of fish. When placed in water, they swim around like little fish, adding a touch of childlike fun to the whole dish-making process.

Ingredients

A

- 5 oz naked oat noodles
- ¼ tsp sesame oil
- 2 tsp brown rice vinegar
- 2 tsp soy sauce
- ¼ tsp salt

B

- 2 oz fried yellow soybean tempeh
- 1 tomato
- 1 tsp vegetable oil
- 1 Tbsp sweet peas

Instructions

❶ Use set A to make the noodle dressing. Mix sesame oil, brown rice vinegar, soy sauce, and salt in a small bowl. Boil the naked oat noodles in boiling water for 10 to 15 minutes. Mix them thoroughly with the noodle dressing once cooked.

❷ For set B, chop the fried tempeh into pieces. Brush a layer of oil on a frying pan and fry the chopped tomato until cooked. Cook the sweet peas until done.

❸ Assemble all the ingredients and serve.

Tip

Method for frying tempeh: Mix whole wheat flour with water to make a batter. Slice the yellow soybean tempeh, coat with the batter, and fry in oil until golden brown.

Wild Vegetable Purple Rice Balls

Purple rice is soft, sticky, and fragrant when cooked. Combine the cooked rice with seasonal spring vegetables from the wild to make rice balls, and top them off with the rich, savory taste of traditional soy sauce. Arranged neatly in a lunch box, these plump rice balls make for the most delightful spring afternoon when taken under a flowering tree to enjoy with a pot of freshly brewed floral tea.

Ingredients

- ½ oz wild shepherd's purse
- ½ oz seaweed seasoning
- 3 oz tricolor brown rice
- 2 oz white quinoa
- 1 Tbsp soy sauce
- 2 tsp sesame oil
- several sheets of seaweed
- ½ tsp hemp seeds

Instructions

❶ Rinse the quinoa and brown rice, and soak the rice for 4 to 8 hours. Add water 1 cm above the level of the rice, then boil the quinoa in a pot for about 15 minutes and the rice for 20 minutes until done, or cook them with a rice cooker using its brown rice setting.

❷ Rinse the shepherd's purse and blanch them in boiling water for about 3 to 5 minutes. Drain the excess water and chop finely.

❸ Add the chopped shepherd's purse to the cooked quinoa and brown rice, and mix them well with the seaweed seasoning, soy sauce, and sesame oil.

❹ Use a mold (or just your hands) to shape the rice into balls or triangles. Wrap each rice ball with a sheet of seaweed and sprinkle with hemp seeds before serving.

hemp seeds

Wild Rice and Cauliflower Salad

Wild rice is actually an interesting ingredient. It thrives in warm and humid environments, often growing in shallow water ditches or low-lying marshy areas. It is three to four times longer than rice, yet its carbohydrate content is quite low. Paired with roasted cauliflower, along with the high-quality fats from nuts, protein from kidney beans, and vitamins from kale, it makes for a beautiful and healthy winter salad option.

Ingredients

A
- 8 small florets of cauliflower
- 2 tsp coconut oil

B
- ½ oz wild rice
- 5 white kidney beans
- 6 red kidney beans
- ½ oz kale
- 6 almonds
- ½ c vinaigrette (see page 24 for recipe)
- 4 pansy flowers (optional)

Instructions

❶ For set A, wash the cauliflower florets, toss them with coconut oil, and place them in the oven. Bake at 150 ℃ for 10 to 12 minutes.

❷ For set B, soak the wild rice for about 4 hours beforehand. Add water 1 cm above the level of the rice, then boil it in a pot for approximately 30 minutes until done, or cook it with a rice cooker using its brown rice setting. Soak the red kidney beans and white kidney beans for 8 hours, then cook them in a pressure cooker for 30 minutes. Wash the kale thoroughly and shake off water.

❸ Combine all ingredients together and drizzle with vinaigrette. When plating, decorate with pansy flowers if desired.

wild rice

Vegetarian Curry
Wild Rice Bowl

When I first encountered wild rice, I was worried that they would be tough and indigestible because of the hard, black shell covering them. However, peeling away the outer shell, I discovered that the rice inside was incredibly delicate and pure white. Once cooked, it emitted a fragrant aroma and had a smooth, non-sticky texture that was both refreshing and moist, with a delightful fragrance. Paired with warm and rich vegetarian curry, the broth enveloping the pristine rice made it irresistible.

Ingredients

- 2 oz red kidney beans
- 1 oz white kidney beans
- 1½ oz baby pumpkin
- 1½ oz carrot
- 1 Tbsp vegetable oil
- ½ oz vegetarian curry block
- ½ oz wild rice
- dash of white sesame

Instructions

❶ Soak the wild rice for about 4 hours beforehand. Add water 1 cm above the level of the rice, then boil it in a pot for approximately 30 minutes until done, or cook it with a rice cooker using its brown rice setting. Soak the red kidney beans and white kidney beans for 8 hours, then cook them in a pressure cooker for 30 minutes until done.

❷ Dice the carrot and baby pumpkin. In a soup pot, heat the vegetable oil and stir-fry the carrot and pumpkin until partially cooked, then add enough water to cover the ingredients. Once the water boils, add the red kidney beans, white kidney beans, and curry block, and simmer until the soup thickens.

❸ According to your taste, pour the vegetarian curry over the wild rice, sprinkle with a few white sesame for decoration and serve.

Oatmeal Pumpkin Soup with Walnut Bread

The rich aroma of oats, the unique fragrance of coconut milk, and the sweet aroma of autumn pumpkin are all comforting scents for me. Combining them together warms both the heart and the stomach.

Ingredients

- ⅙ c instant oatmeal
- 1 c coconut milk
- 4 oz pumpkin
- a pinch of salt
- 2 slices of walnut bread

Instructions

❶ Peel the pumpkin and cut it into chunks. Steam the pumpkin chunks in a steamer for 15 to 20 minutes until they are cooked and soft. Then, mash them into puree.

❷ In a saucepan, bring the instant oatmeal and coconut milk to a boil, stirring until well combined and the oatmeal is cooked and soft. Then, add the prepared pumpkin puree and mix well. Just before serving, add a pinch of salt to taste.

❸ Serve with your favorite bread and enjoy!

Chapter Three
Legumes and Seeds

As a practitioner of a whole plant-based diet, I've often been asked where I get my protein and fat if I don't eat meat, eggs, and dairy. For every vegetarian, the intake of high-quality protein and fats is particularly important in the context of a balanced plant-based diet. The legumes and seeds introduced in this chapter are essential sources for supplementing protein and healthy fats in my daily cooking.

China is the birthplace of soybeans, with a history of cultivation dating back 5,000 years. It is also the earliest developer and producer of bean products. Common examples include tofu, dried tofu, tofu skin, and fried bean curds. Besides soybeans, other beans like red beans and black beans offer even more diverse nutritional profiles. This variety allows us to enjoy delicious meals while efficiently and comprehensively obtaining the protein our bodies need.

When it comes to consuming high-quality fatty acids, seeds are the top choice. Examples include raw pumpkin seeds, hemp seeds, almonds, and cashews. I usually consume seeds directly in their raw form, produced through natural farming methods. Whether as a daily snack or sprinkled onto dishes, they effortlessly meet the body's daily needs for protein and fatty acids, eliminating concerns about inadequate intake.

Broad Bean Mash Veggie Bowl

When I was young, one of my favorite things to do was shelling broad beans in the spring. I would often bring a small stool and sit in the yard, carefully shelling each plump broad bean from its vibrant green pod. Before I knew it, I would have a basket full of them. Cooked broad beans have a soft and buttery texture, with a rich bean flavor. When paired with crisp salad greens, they create a unique and refreshing taste experience.

Ingredients

A
- 2 oz whole wheat flour
- 4 oz firm tofu
- 1 oz diced shiitake mushrooms
- ¼ tsp salt
- 1 Tbsp soy sauce
- 1 Tbsp grape seed oil

B
- 7 oz shelled broad beans
- ¼ tsp salt
- 3 Tbsp olive oil

C
- 1 potato
- 4 asparagus spears
- ½ oz kale
- dash of arugula
- 7 to 8 grapes
- 5 almonds
- ¼ oz pumpkin seeds
- ½ oz purple cabbage
- 1 tsp vinaigrette (see page 24 for recipe)

Instructions

❶ Use set A to make the tofu mushroom patties. Drain the firm tofu using cheesecloth to remove excess moisture, then crumble it. Mix together the whole wheat flour, crumbled tofu, diced shiitake mushrooms, salt, and soy sauce until well combined. Brush a layer of oil onto a skillet and fry the mixture until both sides are golden brown.

❷ Use set B to make the broad bean mash. Cook the fresh broad beans in boiling water for 15 to 20 minutes, then peel them. Place the peeled broad beans in a food processor along with salt and olive oil, and blend until smooth.

❸ For set C, prepare the other vegetable accompaniments. Cut the potato into chunks and the asparagus spears into segments. Brush them with oil and place them in the oven to roast for about 15 minutes. Wash and dry the kale, arugula, and grapes. Shred the purple cabbage and toss it with a bit of vinaigrette.

❹ Assemble all the ingredients and serve.

Turmeric Tofu Rice

The soft and tender tofu resembles a blank canvas, and this time I've used turmeric powder as a paintbrush, giving it a warm golden hue. I then garnish it with vibrant green rocket leaves, creating a dish that evokes thoughts of spring.

Ingredients

A

- 3 oz silken tofu
- 1 shiitake mushroom
- ¼ oz rocket leaves
- 1 Tbsp vegetable oil
- ½ tsp turmeric powder
- 2 tsp soy sauce
- ¼ tsp salt

B

- 2 oz five-color brown rice
- ¼ beetroot
- ⅓ oz pickled young stems of leaf mustard
- ¼ avocado
- dash of chia seeds
- ⅓ oz pumpkin seeds
- ½ tsp roasted seaweed flakes
- 2 slices of radish
- 2 tsp vinaigrette (see page 24 for recipe)
- 2 tsp vegetable oil

Instructions

❶ Use set A to make the turmeric tofu. Crumble the silken tofu, slice the shiitake mushroom and wash the rocket leaves. In a frying pan, heat the oil. Add the sliced mushroom and sauté until fragrant. Then, add the crumbled tofu, rocket leaves, and turmeric powder in succession. Finally, add salt and soy sauce, stir-fry briefly, and then remove from the heat.

❷ For set B, soak the five-color brown rice for 4 to 8 hours. Add water 1 cm above the level of the rice, then boil it for about 20 minutes until done, or cook it with a rice cooker using its brown rice setting. Slice the beetroot into strips and stir-fry with vegetable oil. Wash and dry the pickled young stems of leaf mustard. Slice the avocado and prepare the vegetable combination. Drizzle with some vinaigrette.

❸ Assemble all the ingredients and serve.

Tofu Vegetable Patties

As a dedicated practitioner of a whole plant-based diet, I have a special fondness for tofu. It provides me with ample creative opportunities in cooking. In this dish, I crumble firm tofu, which has a dense texture, and combine it with fresh shiitake mushrooms. After frying them, the crispy exterior and tender interior, along with the fragrant aroma of mushrooms and tofu, present a unique tofu experience.

Ingredients

A

- 3 oz shiitake mushrooms
- 11 oz firm tofu
- 2 tsp salt
- 3 oz whole wheat flour
- 1 oz breadcrumbs
- 1 c frying oil

B

- 1 oz kale
- 1 fig
- ¼ avocado
- 1 walnut kernel
- 1 tsp sesame paste
- 1 tsp tomato sauce
- ½ tsp roasted seaweed flakes

Instructions

❶ Use set A to make the shiitake mushroom tofu patties. Chop the mushrooms, drain the firm tofu using cheesecloth to remove excess moisture, then crumble it. In a large bowl, combine the chopped shiitake mushrooms, crumbled tofu, whole wheat flour, and salt. Mix all the ingredients together until well combined. Shape the mixture into patties, each weighing approximately 3½ oz, and flatten them into round discs. Spread out the breadcrumbs in a shallow dish, then coat both sides of each patty with breadcrumbs.

❷ Heat vegetable oil in a frying pan. Once the oil is hot, reduce the heat to low and carefully add the tofu patties coated with breadcrumbs into the pan. Fry them until both sides are golden brown.

❸ For set B, layer the kale on the bottom of a plate, then place the sliced tofu patties on top. Drizzle with sesame paste and tomato sauce, sprinkle with roasted seaweed flakes. Finally, plate the fig, avocado and walnut pieces to the top.

Rainbow Tofu Salad with Mushroom Oil

The smooth and tender silken tofu can be eaten raw. As a native of Hunan Province, I particularly enjoy sauces with tangy and spicy flavors, and when they are paired with seasonal fruits and vegetables, this tofu dish is not only appetizing but also visually delightful in the hot summer weather.

Ingredients

A

- 1 Tbsp mushroom oil
- 1 tsp balsamic vinegar
- 2 tsp soy sauce
- ½ tsp sesame
- ½ tsp salt

B

- 7 oz silken tofu
- ¼ avocado
- 3 to 4 blueberries
- 2 to 3 cherry tomatoes in different colors

Instructions

❶ Use set A to make the mushroom oil dressing. Mix together the mushroom oil, balsamic vinegar, soy sauce, sesame and salt in a small bowl or glass jar until well combined.

❷ For ingredients B, peel and slice the avocado. Wash the cherry tomatoes and shake off water, then cut them in half. Arrange them on top of the silken tofu. You can either cut the blueberries in half or place them whole on top of the tofu. Drizzle the prepared mushroom oil dressing over the tofu and toppings.

Tips

The mushroom oil can be prepared as follows:

Ingredients: 7 oz mushrooms (such as oyster mushrooms, porcini mushrooms), 7 oz vegetable oil

Use mushrooms such as oyster mushrooms, porcini mushrooms, and shiitake mushrooms. Wash them thoroughly and drain off water. Chop the mushrooms. Heat vegetable oil in a pan until hot, then reduce the heat to low. Add the chopped mushrooms to the hot oil and fry them until crispy. The fragrant mushroom oil can be used in various sauces and adds delicious flavor.

Rice with Tofu Patties

This is a sweet and sour dish where brown sugar is used instead of white sugar to make the sauce, giving it an added depth of flavor with the unique caramel notes of brown sugar. The tangy and sweet sauce permeates the crispy tofu cutlets, which are served with a generous serving of warm brown rice. With simple ingredients, this dish brings layers of deliciousness.

Ingredients

A

- 7 oz firm tofu
- ¼ tsp salt
- 1 Tbsp soy sauce
- 3½ oz whole wheat flour
- 10 Tbsp purified water
- 1 oz breadcrumbs

B

- 2 tsp brown rice vinegar
- 2 Tbsp soy sauce
- 2 tsp brown sugar
- 2 tsp cornstarch
- 13 Tbsp purified water
- 2 tsp vegetable oil

C

- ½ bowl of brown rice
- 5 asparagus spears
- 1 tsp olive oil

Instructions

❶ Use set A to make the tofu patties. Rinse the firm tofu thoroughly, then marinate it with salt and soy sauce for about 15 to 20 minutes. Mix whole wheat flour with purified water to make a batter. Dip the marinated tofu into the batter, ensuring it is evenly coated, then coat it with breadcrumbs. Place the coated tofu patties into an air fryer at 180 °C for 15 minutes. If you don't have an air fryer, you can heat 1 cup of vegetable oil in a frying pan over medium heat. Once hot, reduce the heat to low and add the breaded tofu patties. Fry them until both sides are golden brown.

❷ Use set B to make the seasoning sauce. Heat vegetable oil in a saucepan, add brown rice vinegar, soy sauce, brown sugar, cornstarch, and purified water to the saucepan. Simmer the sauce over low heat until it thickens.

❸ For set C, soak the brown rice for 4 to 8 hours. Add water 1 cm above the level of the rice, then boil it in a pot for approximately 20 minutes until done, or cook it with a rice cooker using its brown rice setting. Heat a small amount of olive oil in a pan over low heat and fry the asparagus spears until cooked. Spread the cooked brown rice on the bottom, place the tofu patties cut into pieces on top, and drizzle with the prepared sauce.

Vegan Vegetable Wraps

Dried tofu is a nutritious, low-fat, and healthy food with a resilient texture. Eating it can also provide a strong sense of satiety. Blanched in water, along with various vegetables of your choice, it is a quick and delicious dish I often choose during my fat-reduction period.

Ingredients

A

- 2 oz dried tofu
- 2 oz cucumber
- 2 oz sweet potato
- ½ oz purple cabbage
- ½ oz lettuce
- 6 pieces whole wheat wraps

B

- 2 oz fresh cashews
- 2 Tbsp plant-based milk
- ¼ tsp lemon juice
- ⅕ oz nutritional yeast powder
- ¼ tsp salt
- 2 tsp maple syrup

Instructions

❶ For set A, start by making the vegan vegetable wraps. Boil the dried tofu for 5 minutes, then cut it into long strips. Cut the cucumber and sweet potato into long strips as well. Wash and dry the purple cabbage and lettuce, then finely shred the purple cabbage. Heat the wraps in a frying pan. Wrap the prepared vegetables in the wraps, then cut them in half.

❷ Use set B to prepare the sauce. Soak the cashews in hot water for 30 minutes, then drain them. Put the cashews along with the other ingredients into a food processor and blend until smooth and creamy.

❸ Drizzle the sauce over the vegan vegetable wraps and serve.

Plant-Based Sour Soup Rice Noodles with Tempeh

When the weather cools down, I usually make a large bowl of tangy and delicious rice noodles with tomatoes. For accompaniment, I choose tempeh, which is commonly stocked in my pantry. Tempeh is rich in probiotics beneficial for the digestive system. It has a firm texture and a solid taste, which balances well with other ingredients and adds a nutty flavor to the dish.

Ingredients

A

- 1 large tomato
- 1 Tbsp vegetable oil
- 1 Tbsp soy sauce
- 2 c pure vegetable broth (see page 25 for recipe)
- ½ oz dried rice noodles
- a pinch of salt

B

- 3 pieces tempeh
- ¼ oz green peas
- ¼ oz black fungus
- ¼ oz corn kernels
- 1 button mushroom
- 1 piece dried bean curd stick
- moderate amount of chili oil

Instructions

❶ For set A, cook the dried rice noodles in boiling water for about 10 to 15 minutes until tender. Peel and chop the large tomato. Heat a little vegetable oil in a pot, add the chopped tomato, stir-fry, then add the vegetable broth and bring to a boil. Add soy sauce and the cooked rice noodles, sprinkle with a pinch of salt to make the tomato broth base.

❷ For set B, fry the tempeh until both sides are crispy. Blanch the green peas, black fungus, corn kernels, button mushroom, and dried bean curd stick in boiling water until cooked. Combine all the ingredients together, and add chili oil according to personal taste.

Tip

Try to buy green peppers with thin skins and thick flesh, as they tend to have a more intense aroma. These green peppers are more likely to have a good texture and a lower level of spiciness.

Stir-Fried Tempeh with Green Peppers

Green pepper is a versatile ingredient in the kitchen. Unlike other spicy peppers, green peppers offer a mild heat while retaining the rich aroma of peppers, adding a crisp and refreshing taste like that of vegetables and fruits, pairing well with the tender texture of tempeh.

Ingredients

- 5 oz green peppers
- 3 oz yellow soybean tempeh
- 2 Tbsp vegetable oil
- ¼ tsp salt
- 2 tsp vegetarian oyster sauce
- ½ tsp white sesame

Instructions

❶ After washing the green peppers, slice them into pieces. Cut the yellow soybean tempeh into cubes.

❷ Heat oil in a pan, then add the green peppers followed by the tempeh. Stir-fry, then add salt and vegetarian oyster sauce. Once cooked, sprinkle some white sesame before serving.

yellow soybean tempeh

Fried Rice with Dried Bean Curd Stick and Pickles

Dried bean curd stick is formed on the surface of boiled soy milk. Skillful chefs will skillfully scoop it out from the boiling pot by hand and hang it on a tall rack to air dry naturally for preservation. After air-drying, the bean curd stick develops numerous small and dense pores inside. Paired with appetizing pickled vegetables, each pore of the bean curd stick absorbs the flavorful broth. With just a light bite, the tender and smooth texture fills the mouth with a fresh and fragrant taste.

Ingredients

- ⅓ oz dried bean curd stick
- ⅓ oz pickled lentils
- ¼ oz kale
- 1½ oz brown rice
- ½ oz tricolor quinoa
- 1 Tbsp soy sauce
- 2 tsp grapeseed oil
- 2 slices of avocado
- ¼ tsp sesame seaweed flakes
- ¼ fig

Tip

The pickled lentils are prepared as follows: After washing fresh lentils, blanch them in boiling water for a moment, then drain off the water. Lay each bean flat and place them in the sun to dry for a day before consuming.

Instructions

❶ Soak the dried bean curd stick in water until soft, then cut it into small pieces. Slice the pickled lentils into thin shreds. Rinse the quinoa and brown rice, and soak the rice for 4 to 8 hours. Add water 1 cm above the level of the rice, then boil the quinoa in a pot for about 15 minutes and the rice for 20 minutes until done, or cook them with a rice cooker using its brown rice setting.

❷ In a frying pan, heat the grapeseed oil, then add the dried bean curd stick pieces and shredded dried lentils, stir-fry. Add the cooked brown rice and quinoa, as well as the kale leaves. Stir-fry over low heat, adding soy sauce. Once cooked, sprinkle with sesame seaweed flakes before serving.

❸ Slice the avocado and cut the fig into pieces. Assemble all the ingredients and serve.

Red Bean Lychee Ice Dessert

Red beans originate from China and have been popular with people there since ancient times. Chinese literati also love to express lovesickness using red beans in their poetry and literary works. The combination of unsweetened red bean paste and sweet lychee creates this healthy and delicious dessert. With each bite, the juice of the lychee, the smoothness of the red bean paste, and the crunchiness of the ice chips create a refreshing explosion of flavors in the mouth during the hot summer days.

Ingredients

- ½ oz red beans
- 8 lychees

Instructions

❶ The red beans need to be soaked for 8 hours in advance. If the temperature is high in the summer, they should be soaked in the refrigerator. After soaking, wash the beans, drain the water, and cook them in a pressure cooker until soft. Once cooked, blend them into a paste using a food processor. If you don't have a pressure cooker, you can also directly purchase ready-made red bean paste.

❷ After peeling and removing the seeds from the lychees, fill them with the red bean paste using a small spoon. Place them in the freezer for about 1 hour before serving.

Tip

Before consuming, let the red bean lychees sit at room temperature for about 5 minutes to soften slightly for a better texture.

Red Bean Cashew Milk

Tip

Don't discard the leftover residue filtered out. It is rich in nutrients and can be used to make pancakes or other baked goods.

Every week, I dedicate a day to cooking beans. I cook all the beans I plan to eat for the week at once, then portion them and store them in the freezer. Pre-cooked beans can be quickly used to make daily servings of plant-based milk, providing you with a quick and convenient source of plant protein.

Ingredients

- 1 oz cooked red beans
- ¼ oz raw cashews
- 1 tsp instant oatmeal
- 1 small banana
- 1 c warm water

Instructions

❶ Put all ingredients into a high-speed blender and blend until smooth.

❷ Strain the mixture through cheesecloth or a fine mesh strainer to remove any remaining residue.

Warm Salad with Red Kidney Beans and Sweet Potato

Red kidney beans are rich in dietary fiber and are one of the ingredients commonly used to supplement iron intake in daily diets. I love the sticky texture of cooked red kidney beans, so I often cook a large batch at once. I portion them according to the amount I'll use for each meal and store them in the freezer. When I want to eat them, I simply take out a packet and thaw it, restoring the red kidney beans to their original texture effortlessly.

Ingredients

- 1 small sweet potato
- ½ oz red kidney beans
- 1 oz purple pakchoi cabbage stalks
- 4 slices of avocado
- 2 tsp vegetable oil
- 3 slices of apple
- ½ oz tricolor quinoa
- 1 Tbsp peanut sesame sauce (see page 23 for recipe)

Instructions

❶ After peeling the sweet potato and washing it clean, cut it into small pieces. Brush a layer of oil on a baking tray, then place the sweet potato in the oven at 180 ℃ for about 10 to 15 minutes. Boil the tricolor quinoa in a pot for approximately 15 minutes.

❷ Soak the red kidney beans in water for 4 hours in advance. After rinsing them clean with water, put them in a pressure cooker and cook for about 30 minutes. Wash the purple pakchoi cabbage stalks. Heat vegetable oil in a pot and blanch the leaves until they are cooked.

❸ Slice the avocado and the apple. Assemble all the ingredients and drizzle with peanut sesame sauce.

red kidney beans

Edamame with Mushroom Sauce

Tips

If you like a spicy taste in the mushroom sauce, you can add some chili powder. Since soybean paste and soy sauce contain salt, you can adjust the amount of salt according to your taste preference. The mushroom sauce goes well with rice or noodles and is delicious either way.

Edamame are very particular about their ingredients. It is essential to choose fresh and tender ones in season so they can easily absorb flavors when cooked.

This dish has a simple preparation method, but the quality of the ingredients is crucial. The unshelled edamame retain their tender texture inside the pods. Because of their quality, simply boiling them in water brings out the aroma of the edamame. Adding mushroom sauce made in winter further enhances the flavor and texture.

Ingredients

A
- ½ oz dried shiitake mushrooms
- ½ oz dried flower mushrooms
- ½ oz dried tea tree mushrooms
- 1 Tbsp soybean paste
- 1 Tbsp vegetarian oyster sauce
- 1 Tbsp soy sauce
- ½ c rapeseed oil

B
- 10 oz fresh edamame
- ¼ c mushroom sauce
- ¼ tsp salt
- ⅕ oz cinnamon stick
- 1 piece of bay leaf

Instructions

❶ Use set A to make the mushroom sauce. Soak the dried shiitake mushrooms, dried flower mushrooms, and dried tea tree mushrooms in water for about 3 to 4 hours. After soaking, drain the water and chop the mushrooms. Heat rapeseed oil in a pot, add the chopped mushrooms, then add soybean paste, vegetarian oyster sauce, soy sauce, and stir-fry until well combined.

❷ For set B, trim the two ends of the fresh edamame, wash them, and then boil them in water until cooked. Add salt, cinnamon stick, and bay leaf to the boiling water, then reduce the heat and simmer until well-flavored. Once the edamame are cooked, add the mushroom sauce and mix well before serving.

Green Soybean Sauce Eggplant Pasta

In southern China, edamame is best savored in early autumn as it is usually harvested during this time. Freshly picked and shelled edamame beans are plump, tender, fragrant, and vibrantly green. Stir-fry, stew, boil, or cook them any way and they taste marvelous. Make them into a pesto, toss in the pasta, serve with pine nuts and pan-fried eggplant, and appreciate the wonderful texture of different ingredients fusing in your mouth with every bite.

Ingredients

A

• 3 oz edamame beans
• 2 tsp yeast powder
• 2 tsp olive oil
• ⅕ c almond milk
• 1 tsp dried basil leaves

B

• ½ eggplant
• 2 oz fusilli pasta
• 1 Tbsp vegetable oil
• 1 Tbsp pine nuts
• ¼ tsp salt
• ¼ c water
• ½ tsp hemp seeds

Instructions

❶ Use set A to make the edamame pesto. Cook the edamame beans before combining them with the yeast powder, olive oil, almond milk, and dried basil leaves in a food processor, and blend into a smooth sauce.

❷ For set B, cut the eggplant into round slices, place them in a frying pan coated with a layer of oil, and pan-fry over low heat. Cook the pasta in boiling water. Sauté the pine nuts in the vegetable oil, add the cooked pasta, and stir in the edamame pesto. Add a little water and salt if the result is too dry.

❸ Assemble all the ingredients, sprinkle with hemp seeds before serving.

Tomato Spaghetti with Tempeh

Tips

Chickpeas can be soaked overnight in advance, and rinsed the next morning before cooking. It is advisable to refrigerate them during summer, when temperatures are high.

Similar legume ingredients can be soaked and cooked for multiple servings at one time. Once cooked, leftovers can be stored in the refrigerator or freezer and take them out whenever you want to serve them next time.

Tomatoes are one of the most versatile ingredients, and tomato spaghetti is a classic among pasta varieties. Whip up a thick sauce with tempeh and tomatoes, and enjoy how the sweet and sour gravy envelops the soft yet firm texture of the tempeh chunks, making each strand of spaghetti rich and flavorful.

Ingredients

A

- 1 tomato
- 2 oz tempeh
- 1 Tbsp olive oil
- ¼ tsp black pepper
- ¼ tsp salt
- ¼ oz basil
- 1 c pure vegetable broth (see page 25 for recipe)

B

- 2 oz whole wheat spaghetti

C

- 4 brussels sprouts
- 11 chickpeas
- 1 walnut
- 3 blueberries
- ½ avocado
- 1 strawberry
- ⅕ oz endives
- 2 tsp vinaigrette (see page 24 for recipe)

Instructions

❶ Use set A to make the pasta sauce. Peel the tomato and dice both the tomato and tempeh. In a frying pan, add some oil to sauté the tempeh until brown and crisp before adding the diced tomatoes to stir-fry. Add a moderate amount of pure vegetable broth and seasonings.

❷ For set B, cook the spaghetti in boiling water and toss it with the completed pasta sauce.

❸ Set C is a combined platter of fruits and vegetables. Parboil the brussels sprouts before putting them in the oven to roast. Soak the chickpeas overnight before cooking them in a pressure cooker. Slice the avocado. Rinse the blueberries and endives and shake them dry. Combine all the fruits and vegetables into a salad and drizzle with vinaigrette.

❹ Assemble all the ingredients and serve.

Plant-Based Bowl with Chickpeas Fried Rice

Fried rice is a particularly accommodating dish. When you're starving and in need of a quick meal, just open your refrigerator, grab some ingredients, and fry yourself a tasty meal with minimal seasonings and minimum fuss. In this recipe, soft, chewy chickpeas intertwine with fresh, plump shiitake mushrooms, alongside refreshingly juicy fruits and vegetables, to stir up a meal that is harmonious in taste, yet distinct in individual flavors, and can be prepared in no time.

Ingredients

A

- ⅓ oz chickpeas
- 2 oz brown rice
- ½ oz kale stems
- 2 shiitake mushrooms
- 1 Tbsp soy sauce
- 2 tsp vegetable oil

B

- 1 oz dried tofu
- dash of red onions

C

- 5 cashew nuts
- ½ avocado
- 1 walnut
- 1 kiwi
- ½ oz endives
- 2 tsp vinaigrette (see page 24 for recipe)

Instructions

❶ Use set A to make the fried rice. Soak the brown rice for 4 to 8 hours before cooking. Add water 1 cm above the level of the rice, then boil the rice in a pot for about 20 minutes, or cook them with a rice cooker using its brown rice setting. Rinse the shiitake mushrooms and cut into slices. Heat a little vegetable oil in a pan. Sauté the shiitake mushrooms and kale stems until cooked, then add the cooked brown rice and chickpeas, and stir-fry before adding the soy sauce.

❷ For set B, cut the dried tofu into slices and the red onions into thin strips. Grease a pan and roast them in the oven for 5 minutes.

❸ For set C, slice the avocado and kiwi, rinse the endives and shake them dry, sprinkle with walnuts, and drizzle vinaigrette over the vegetables.

❹ Assemble all the ingredients and serve.

Veggie Bowl with Black Bean Tempeh

I always enjoy trying various types of ingredients to make each meal look different in the process of exploring food. This time, I experimented with making a veggie bowl using tempeh made from black beans, which provides a stronger chewiness compared to regular tempeh. I paired it with pre-marinated pickled vegetables, creating a nutritious and satisfying meal.

Ingredients

A

- 2 oz brown rice
- ¼ oz raisins
- 2 tsp coconut oil

B

- 4 slices of black bean tempeh
- 1 Tbsp soy sauce
- 1 Tbsp grapeseed oil
- a pinch of salt

C

- 9 asparagus spears
- ½ oz rocket leaves
- ⅓ oz pumpkin seeds
- moderate amount of any pickled vegetables
- dash of hemp seeds
- a pinch of salt
- a pinch of black pepper

Instructions

❶ For set A, soak the brown rice for 4 to 8 hours. Then, add water (1 cm above the level of the rice), raisins, and coconut oil to a pot, and cook for about 20 minutes until done, or cook them with a rice cooker using its brown rice setting.

❷ For set B, place the black bean tempeh in a bowl and add soy sauce, salt, and grapeseed oil. Mix well and marinate for 10 to 15 minutes. Then, heat a small amount of grapeseed oil in a frying pan over low heat and pan-fry the tempeh until crispy on both sides.

❸ For set C, brush a layer of oil in a pan and pan-fry the asparagus spears until cooked. Season with salt and black pepper according to taste. Wash the rocket leaves. You can choose your favorite pickled vegetables to enhance the flavor. In the picture, homemade pickled ginger with gorgon stems are used.

❹ Assemble all the ingredients and serve.

Chapter Four
Root Vegetables

When it comes to root vegetables, the first ones that may come to mind are potatoes, yams, and sweet potatoes, which are deeply buried in the soil. Due to their high starch content, they have been used as staple foods in many countries around the world throughout history. However, there are actually many more root vegetables that grow in the mountains, fields, and lakes. They not only provide carbohydrates as an alternative to whole grains for plant-based bowls but also provide us with the fiber and vitamins we need daily. They are truly versatile ingredients.

In this chapter, I would like to share with you not only those familiar root vegetables but also many traditional root vegetables that originate from the mountains and fields of China. Like the "eight water immortals" that grow underwater and are closely tied to the seasons, the energy-rich superfood turmeric, and the Chinese-flavored arrowhead and fish mint. Each season brings its own vegetable, with its unique flavor and story. These mountain and field flavors can also heal our bodies and minds.

Water Chestnut Dumplings

Tip

Steps to wrap a dumpling:

1. Prepare some dumpling wrappers.

2. Take a dumpling wrapper, place some filling in the middle.

3. Moisten the edge of the wrapper with some water for better adhesion, fold one side over.

4. Seal it in your preferred shape, be careful not to expose the filling.

Water chestnuts are sweet, juicy, and crunchy when eaten raw, making them one of the most precious fruits from my childhood that I couldn't bear to finish. Adding water chestnuts to the dumpling filling adds a fresh and sweet taste. With every bite, the juice dominates your entire mouth, leaving a lingering flavor that you'll savor.

Ingredients

A

- 3 oz water chestnuts
- 1 king oyster mushroom
- 1 Tbsp vegetable oil
- 1 oz firm tofu
- 1 Tbsp soy sauce
- 3 oz dumpling wrappers

B

- 12 oz kombu broth (see page 25 for recipe)
- 2 tsp brown rice vinegar
- 2 tsp soy sauce
- 1 tsp sesame oil
- ½ tsp sesame

C

- ¼ oz tofu
- 1 milk cabbage
- 1 tsp vegetable oil

Instructions

❶ Use set A to make water chestnut dumplings. Peel and dice the fresh water chestnuts. Dice the king oyster mushroom. Heat vegetable oil in a frying pan, sauté the king oyster mushroom until cooked. Squeeze the moisture out of the firm tofu using cheesecloth, then crumble it. After that, put the water chestnuts and king oyster mushroom into a food processor and blend them. Mix the blended mixture with the crumbled tofu and soy sauce to make the dumpling filling. Once the filling is ready, start wrapping the dumplings (refer to the steps in the tip). Boil the dumplings in boiling water until they float, indicating they are cooked.

❷ Use set B to prepare the soup base. Pour the kombu broth into a pot and bring it to a boil. Then, add the brown rice vinegar and soy sauce. Just before serving, add the sesame oil. Pour the soup over the cooked dumplings in a bowl, and sprinkle some sesame seeds on top.

❸ For ingredients C, fry the tofu with oil until cooked, and boil the milk cabbage in boiling water until tender.

❹ Assemble all the above and serve.

Veggie Bowl with Red Curried Winter Bamboo Shoots

Bamboo shoots have a history of thousands of years in China. The best time to enjoy winter bamboo shoots is around the beginning of winter, between early November and late January when the freshest and most tender ones are harvested. Paired with red curry, the bite and richness of the spices accentuate the freshness and crispness of the bamboo shoots. Eating them with rice and vegetables provides one's taste buds with a unique treat, making this a food I must have every winter.

Ingredients

A

- 1 oz brown rice
- ½ oz black soybeans
- 1 Tbsp soy sauce
- 2 tsp sesame oil

B

- 3 oz winter bamboo shoots
- 1 Tbsp red curry paste
- 1 Tbsp lemon juice
- 2 Tbsp vegetable oil
- 1 Tbsp soy sauce
- dash of mint leaves
- ⅕ oz minced ginger
- ⅕ oz minced garlic
- ½ c pure vegetable broth (see page 25 for recipe)

Instructions

❶ Make brown rice balls with black soybeans using set A. Rinse the brown rice and soak for 4 to 8 hours. Add water 1 cm above the level of the rice and boil in a pot for about 20 minutes, or cook them with a rice cooker using its brown rice setting. Soak the black soybeans for 4 hours in advance before cooking them in a pressure cooker for about 20 minutes. Add the soy sauce and sesame oil to the cooked black soybeans and brown rice and mix well. Shape the rice into balls. If desired, lay a plastic wrap on your palm to help with the shaping of the rice balls.

❷ Use set B to make red curried winter bamboo shoots. Peel and cut the winter bamboo shoots into chunks, blanch them in boiling water for 15 to 20 minutes to remove their bitterness, and set aside for later use. Add the vegetable oil to a slightly deeper wok, and lightly sauté the minced ginger and garlic before adding the vegetable broth, curry paste, and soy sauce to cook for about 10 minutes. When the broth comes to a boil, add the blanched bamboo shoots and cook for another 10 minutes or so. Add the lemon juice and fresh mint leaves, and allow the broth to thicken and absorbed slightly before removing it from the heat.

(Continued on next page)

C

- 1 oz red cabbage
- 1 oz kale
- ⅓ oz pumpkin seeds
- dash of chia seeds
- ½ avocado
- 1 tsp vinaigrette (see page 24 for recipe)
- dash of black and white sesame

D

- 3 oz red bell peppers
- 1 Tbsp tea seed oil
- a pinch of salt

❸ For set C, plate the halved avocado directly. Use purified water to rinse the red cabbage and kale, and dry them with a salad spinner. Slice the red cabbage into thin strips and break the kale into small pieces. Clean your hands and rub the kale leaves to soften them. After plating, sprinkle with pumpkin seeds, black and white sesame seeds, and chia seeds, then drizzle with vinaigrette and toss well.

❹ Use set D to make roasted bell peppers. Wash the bell peppers, remove the seeds and stems, and slice them into strips. Place the bell pepper strips in a baking tray, brush them with some tea seed oil, and sprinkle a pinch of salt. If you don't have a baking tray, use a frying pan instead. Roast the bell peppers over medium heat for 10 to 15 minutes. Extend the time if you prefer a softer texture. Roll up the roasted bell pepper strips.

❺ Assemble all the ingredients and serve.

Tips

You can cook extra brown rice for the rice balls and freeze the leftovers in a sealed bag. Just defrost and reheat before eating.

Kale leaves are relatively tough; a little rubbing can soften them and make them easier to chew.

Sweet Potato Energy Sandwich

In autumn and winter, when the wind blows and leaves turn yellow, you can often smell the aroma of roasted sweet potatoes from roadside vendors while walking down the street. Sweet potatoes in autumn are the most delicious. When they are baked in the oven until the skin is crispy and the inside is soft, tender, and sweet, the whole kitchen is filled with a warm and comforting aroma.

Ingredients

- 9 oz medium-sized sweet potatoes
- ½ avocado
- 1 oz tempeh
- 2 tsp olive oil
- ¼ tsp sea salt
- 1 tsp soy sauce
- ½ oz pomegranate seeds
- ½ tsp cinnamon powder

Instructions

❶ Wash the sweet potatoes and place them on the middle rack of the oven. Bake at 230 ℃ for 45 minutes until tender. Let them rest for 5 to 10 minutes before removing them for later use.

❷ Mash half of a ripe avocado until smooth.

❸ Cut the tempeh into 0.5-cm cubes. Mix olive oil, salt, and soy sauce in a small bowl. Add the diced tempeh to the bowl and marinate for 10 minutes.

❹ Brush a layer of oil in a pan and fry the tempeh pieces until crispy. Cut the baked sweet potatoes in half and spread mashed avocado on each half. Then, add the fried tempeh pieces on top, sprinkle with pomegranate seeds and cinnamon powder.

Tip

The sweet potato sandwich is a very healthy staple food, and it's also an alternative way to enjoy sweet potatoes. The fillings can be varied according to preference.

Salad Bowl with Sweet Potato

Roasted sweet potatoes evoke exclusive memories of autumn and winter seasons, as well as being an excellent choice for a main dish. Paired with various nutritious vegetables, fruits, and nuts, they create a colorful bowl of salad that is both filling and light, making it very suitable for consumption during a weight-loss period.

Ingredients

A

- ½ large sweet potato
- 2 tsp soy yogurt

B

- ½ oz chickpeas
- 1 tsp oil
- ¼ tsp salt

C

- 2 oz blueberries
- 1 fig
- ½ oz endive leaves
- 1 pecan
- ½ oz tricolor quinoa
- ½ passion fruit
- 1 Tbsp vinaigrette (see page 24 for recipe)

Instructions

❶ For set A, wash the sweet potato and place it in a preheated oven at 250 °C for 30 minutes. Once roasted, cut it open and drizzle with the soy yogurt.

❷ Use set B to make crispy chickpeas. Soak the chickpeas in advance, then cook them until tender. Drain them and toss with oil and salt until evenly coated. Place them in the oven and bake for 10 to 15 minutes.

❸ For set C, boil the tricolor quinoa in a pot for about 15 minutes until cooked. Wash and dry the blueberries and endive leaves. Cut open the passion fruit and fig. Assemble all the ingredients and drizzle with vinaigrette.

Tip

Do not soak the spring
roll wrappers for too long
as they may become too
soft for wrapping the
fillings within.

Carrot Spring Rolls with Tangy Citrus Spicy Sauce

Whenever I run out of ideas of what to eat, I always look into my food basket to see what seasonal fruits and vegetables might be available to fill some spring rolls. Fresh, sweet, and crisp carrots are my favorite choice for winter. Rolled up with different fruits that I like, the transparent spring roll wrappers hold a visual feast of bursting colors while the crunchy fillings, accompanied by the sour and spicy dipping sauce, are an absolute delight on the tongue. A double treat indeed!

Ingredients (for 5 rolls)

A

- 1 small carrot
- 1 strawberry
- 1 slice of orange
- 1 slice of banana
- 1 slice of avocado
- 5 Vietnamese spring roll wrappers

B

- 1 oz mandarin orange juice
- 2 tsp maple syrup
- 2 tsp olive oil
- dash of red chili peppers

Instructions

❶ For set A, wash and peel the carrot, then cut it into 5 cm-long strips. Slice the strawberry, orange, banana, and avocado. Soak the spring roll wrappers in water for 3 to 5 seconds, and lay them on a flat plate. Arrange the carrots and accompanying fruit on the lower section of each wrapper, fold them on the sides, then roll it up from the bottom until the ingredients are tightly wrapped.

❷ Use set B to make the spicy citrus sauce. Start by extracting fresh mandarin orange juice, then blend the juice with the chopped chili peppers, maple syrup, and olive oil into an even mix.

Sweet and Sour
Water Chestnuts

Water chestnuts are a delicious gift from the fields and a memory of summer for me. They have a distinct seasonality, with a short time from harvesting to market. It is this brief encounter that makes them unforgettable. They are crisp and refreshing when eaten raw, and soft and glutinous when cooked. No matter how they are prepared, they always carry the sweet taste of my childhood memories.

Ingredients

A

- 8 dried flower mushrooms
- 1 oz raw cashews
- 3 oz fresh water chestnuts
- 1 Tbsp brown rice vinegar
- ¼ tsp salt
- 1 Tbsp maple syrup
- 2 tsp soy sauce
- 3 Tbsp vegetable oil

B

- ½ eggplant
- 2 tsp vegetable oil
- ¼ tsp salt

C

- 1 oz brown rice
- ½ tsp seaweed seasoning with sesame
- ⅕ oz raw pumpkin seeds
- ½ small cucumber
- 2 broccoli florets

Instructions

❶ For set A, soak the dried flower mushrooms in water until they are soft, then set aside. Heat vegetable oil in a pan, then add the fresh water chestnuts, flower mushrooms, and cashews in sequence. Stir-fry them together, then add brown rice vinegar, maple syrup, soy sauce, and a little salt to season.

❷ For set B, wash the eggplant and cut it into thin slices. Brush them lightly with oil and place them in the oven at 150 ℃ for about 12 minutes until cooked. After baking, sprinkle with a little salt, then roll them up.

❸ For set C, soak the brown rice for 4 to 8 hours beforehand. Add water 1 cm above the level of the rice, then boil it in a pot for approximately 20 minutes until done, or cook it with a rice cooker using its brown rice setting. Mix the cooked brown rice with the seaweed seasoning. Slice the cucumber into thin strips and roll them up. Blanch the broccoli florets until cooked. Sprinkle with pumpkin seeds. Assemble all the ingredients and serve.

Tip

The vegetables and fruits inside the pancake crust can be replaced with ones you prefer to create your own combination.

Turmeric Whole Plant-Based Pancake

Turmeric is a powerful healing food, and is considered one of the world's "top ten superfoods." It has been a part of Chinese history for over a thousand years. Its main active compound, curcumin, possesses anti-inflammatory and antioxidant properties. This recipe involves adding turmeric powder to the flour to create a yellow pancake crust. The vibrant yellow crust wraps around a variety of colorful fruits, making it a dessert that looks incredibly appetizing and full of vitality for a delightful afternoon treat.

Ingredients

A

- 7 oz low-gluten flour
- 1 Tbsp maple syrup
- 1 c coconut milk
- ¼ tsp turmeric powder
- ¼ tsp vanilla extract
- ½ tsp black sesame
- 1 Tbsp vegetable oil

B

- 1 oz kale
- 2 to 3 strawberries
- ½ avocado
- 1 Tbsp peanut sesame sauce (see page 23 for recipe)

Instructions

❶ For set A, mix the low-gluten flour, maple syrup, vanilla extract, coconut milk, black sesame, and turmeric powder in a glass bowl to form a relatively thin batter. Brush a non-stick pan with oil and spread the batter into a round pancake shape.

❷ For set B, after washing and drying the kale and strawberries, cut the strawberries and avocado into pieces. First, spread the peanut sesame sauce onto the surface of the pancake crust. Then, layer the kale, strawberries, and avocado on top.

Whole Plant-Based Bowl with Hijiki Seaweed and Water Bamboo

Water bamboo is a unique aquatic vegetable in China, often referred to as the "ginseng of the water." During the summer and autumn seasons, households in the south of the Yangtze River would purchase fresh seasonal water bamboo for cooking. The outer shell of water bamboo is green, while the inside is tender and white. When paired with hijiki seaweed, the combination offers a soft and sweet taste.

Ingredients

A

- 1 oz water bamboo
- ⅕ oz hijiki seaweed
- 1 Tbsp soy sauce
- 2 tsp maple syrup
- ¼ tsp salt
- ¼ c pure vegetable broth (see page 25 for recipe)
- 1 Tbsp vegetable oil

B

- 7 oz mixed brown rice
- 2 tsp brown rice vinegar
- 1 Tbsp seaweed seasoning
- 2 sheets of seaweed
- ¼ oz cooked chickpeas

C

- ¼ avocado
- ¼ oz kale
- ½ small cucumber
- 2 tsp vinaigrette (see page 24 for recipe)

Instructions

❶ Use set A to make stir-fried hijiki seaweed with water bamboo. Soak the hijiki seaweed in advance. Peel the water bamboo and cut them into small chunks. Blanch them in boiling water for 30 seconds to remove oxalic acid. In a pan, add vegetable oil and stir-fry the bamboo shoots and hijiki seaweed. Then, add salt, soy sauce, and maple syrup to season. Before serving, pour in some pure vegetable broth.

❷ Use set B to make brown rice balls. Soak the brown rice for 4 to 8 hours beforehand. Add water 1 cm above the level of the rice, then boil it in a pot for approximately 20 minutes until done, or cook it with a rice cooker using its brown rice setting. Pour the brown rice into a bowl, then add the brown rice vinegar, mixed rice seasoning with seaweed, and cooked chickpeas in sequence and mix well. Lay plastic wrap flat on your palm, shape the seasoned brown rice into your desired shape, and wrap a sheet of seaweed around the bottom of the rice ball.

❸ Use set C to make the side salad. Cut the avocado into chunks. Wash and dry the kale leaves, then slice the cucumber into thin strips and roll them up. Drizzle with vinaigrette.

❹ Assemble all the ingredients and serve.

Yam Sushi

This is a healthy quick snack suitable for people of all ages. The perfect combination of yam and carrot blends the softness of yam with the sweetness of carrot. Without the need for excessive additional seasoning, enjoying the original flavors of the ingredients is delicious enough.

Ingredients

- 1 sheet of seaweed
- 3 oz iron yam
- 3 oz carrot
- 1 Tbsp sushi soy sauce
- 2 tsp vegetable oil

Instructions

❶ Peel off the skin and dirt from the yam. Wash the carrot thoroughly. Steam both over water until soft, then remove and let cool. Peel off the outer skin. Mash the yam and carrot into a paste, and mix in the sushi soy sauce evenly.

❷ Lay the seaweed flat, spread a portion of the yam paste evenly on the sushi mat, roll it into a sushi roll, and moisten the tail end of the seaweed with a little water to seal it.

❸ Cut the sushi roll into sections. Heat a small amount of oil in a flat-bottomed pan until hot, then place the cut sushi pieces into the pan and fry until the surface is crispy.

Yam and Pearl Barley Congee

Yam is one of the most widely known medicinal and food homologous ingredients in China. Cooking yam, pearl barley, and oats together into congee not only yields a soft, sticky, and sweet texture but also carries therapeutic effects, beneficial for the spleen and stomach. Consuming it as breakfast opens up a warm day ahead.

Ingredients

A

- 3 oz yam
- 1½ oz pearl barley
- 1 oz oats
- 1 c water

B

- ¼ avocado
- 1½ oz seedless pomegranate seeds
- 7 blueberries
- 3 blackberries
- ¼ fig
- ¼ tsp chia seeds

Instructions

❶ For set A, peel the yam and cut it into chunks. Soak the pearl barley for 2 hours in advance, then drain the water and set aside. Put the yam chunks, pearl barley, oats, and water into the rice cooker, and cook them with its congee setting. If you don't have a rice cooker, it's best to use a pressure cooker and cook for 30 minutes until the pearl barley are soft and sticky. If you use a regular pot, all ingredients should be cooked for at least 1 hour, and you'll need to stir and add water as needed to prevent the ingredients sticking to the pot.

❷ For set B, slice the avocado and fig. Wash the blueberries and blackberries, then drain them dry. Once the yam congee has cooled, combine all the ingredients.

Yam Mash with Persimmon Sauce

This is a delightful vegetarian dessert that pleases both the eyes and the taste buds. At every picnic, it is always the first to be snatched up. The soft and sticky yam mash blends with coconut milk, emitting a rich coconut aroma. Then, pouring a spoonful of golden sweet persimmon sauce over each snowy white yam ball, making it not only visually appealing but also delicious.

Ingredients

A

- 7 oz iron yam
- 1 Tbsp coconut milk
- ½ oz rice wine

B

- 2 persimmons

Instructions

❶ Use set A to make yam balls. Peel the yam, steam it in a pot for 15 minutes, then lightly mash it. Filter the rice wine and coconut milk through a strainer or cheesecloth, mix well, and add it to the steamed yam. Then mash the yam into a paste, wrap it in plastic wrap, and shape it into balls.

❷ Use set B to make persimmon sauce. Preheat the oven to 180 ℃ , place the persimmons in the oven and roast for 5 to 8 minutes. Peel them, scoop out the flesh with a spoon, and mash it into a paste. Drizzle the persimmon sauce over the yam balls.

Tip

Try to choose ripe persimmons. Roasting them will enhance their sweetness even more.

Taro with Fermented Bean Curd

The texture of taro is delicate and soft, sweet and sticky, and easy to digest. Steamed taro dipped in white sugar is a childhood memory for many Chinese children. In this dish, I use traditional Chinese fermented bean curd as a seasoning to add a fresh and spicy sensation to the mild taro.

Ingredients

A

- 2 oz flavored bean curd
- 1 taro
- ¼ oz fermented bean curd
- 1 tsp soy sauce
- 1 tsp white sesame
- 1 tsp vinegar
- 3 tsp vegetable oil

B

- 2 oz bean sprouts
- dash of sesame oil
- 1 piece of tomato
- ¼ avocado
- dash of kale
- ½ tsp seaweed seasoning
- 2 oz brown rice

Instructions

❶ For set A, steam the taro until cooked. Blanch the flavored bean curd in boiling water for about 3 minutes, then cut it into pieces and set aside. Then, prepare the sauce. In a small bowl, mix together the fermented bean curd, soy sauce, white sesame seeds, and vinegar. Heat the vegetable oil until hot, then pour it over the prepared sauce. Mix the sauce with the chopped taro and flavored bean curd until well combined.

❷ For set B, blanch the bean sprouts in boiling water until tender, then mix them with sesame oil. Fry the tomato in oil for a while. Cut the avocado into chunks. Soak the brown rice for 4 to 8 hours beforehand. Add water 1 cm above the level of the rice, then boil it in a pot for approximately 20 minutes until done, or cook it with a rice cooker using its brown rice setting.

❸ Assemble all the ingredients and serve.

Steamed Dumplings with White Radish and Shredded Tofu Sheet

Tip

Please refer to page 83 for the method of wrapping dumplings.

Steamed dumplings are my favorite way to enjoy dumplings. With thin skin and generous filling, each dumpling becomes translucent and crystal-clear under the steam. The dumpling skin becomes soft yet chewy. Taking a bite, the juicy essence of white radish bursts forth, complemented by the freshness of shredded tofu sheet. It's light yet flavorful, with the ingredients blending perfectly to bring out the essence of the food.

Ingredients

- 7 oz white radish
- 2 oz tofu sheet
- 2 tsp light soy sauce
- 1 tsp dark soy sauce
- ¼ tsp salt
- ¼ tsp sesame oil
- 2 tsp vegetable oil
- 10 dumpling wrappers

Instructions

❶ Grate the white radish into fine strips, sprinkle some salt over it, and let it sit to release water. After it's marinated, squeeze out the excess water. Cut the tofu sheet into fine strips.

❷ Heat oil in a pan, stir-fry the shredded radish and tofu sheet until evenly cooked. Then add some light soy sauce and salt to season, and a few drops of dark soy sauce for color. Once cooked, let it cool down, then add a few drops of sesame oil for fragrance.

❸ Once the filling is prepared, start wrapping the dumplings. Take one dumpling wrapper, place some filling in the middle, moisten the edge of the wrapper with some water for better adhesion, then fold one side over to meet the other, and pinch to seal into your desired shape.

❹ Place the dumplings in a steamer and steam over high heat for 10 to 15 minutes.

shredded tofu sheet

Baked Lily Bulbs with Coconut Oil

The first time I tried baked lily bulbs was at a restaurant. As soon as the lid of the clay pot was lifted, I was drawn in by the tantalizing aroma and amazed to see a whole lily bulb in there. In my memory, lily bulbs always appeared on the dining table as a supporting role in sweet soups. I never imagined that using savory seasonings to prepare lily bulbs, such a naturally sweet ingredient, would be so fitting. Remember to choose plump and tender lily bulbs for the best taste.

Ingredients

- 3 oz fresh lily bulbs
- 1 Tbsp vegetable oil
- ¼ oz fresh rosemary
- 2 tsp vegetarian oyster sauce
- 1 tsp maple syrup
- ¼ c water
- 2 tsp soy sauce
- ¼ tsp salt
- moderate amount of lemon water

Instructions

❶ Clean the lily bulbs, removing any dirt or sand. Place them in some lemon water to prevent oxidation.

❷ In a clay pot, add a layer of oil, then add the lily bulbs and some water. Boil the lily bulbs for 10 minutes.

❸ To make the seasoning sauce, mix salt, maple syrup, soy sauce, vegetable oil, vegetarian oyster sauce, and a small amount of water in a small bowl until well mixed.

❹ Pour the seasoning sauce into the cooked softened lily bulbs. Cover the clay pot with its lid and let it simmer for one minute. Garnish with fresh rosemary.

fresh lily bulbs

Stir-Fried Asparagus with Lily Bulbs

Lily bulbs have a long history of cultivation in China, and their taste varies greatly depending on their origin. Unlike the previous dish of baked lily bulbs, the lily bulbs in this dish require a crispy and sweet taste. Stir-fried with asparagus, they don't need too much seasoning, yet you can still taste the natural goodness of the ingredients.

Ingredients

- 2 oz fresh lily bulbs
- 2 oz asparagus spears
- ½ oz edamame
- 1 Tbsp grapeseed oil
- 2 tsp soy sauce
- ¼ tsp vinegar
- ¼ tsp salt
- 5 to 6 hibiscus flowers (optional)

Instructions

❶ Wash the fresh lily bulbs thoroughly and break them into small florets. Trim the tender parts of the asparagus spears and cut them into segments.

❷ In a frying pan, heat the oil. Add the asparagus spears first, then add the lily bulbs and edamame. Add soy sauce, salt, and vinegar one by one for seasoning, then stir-fry until cooked.

❸ After plating, you can use hibiscus flowers for decoration.

Tip

Lotus root balls can be cooked by steaming or frying. Once prepared, you can freeze them for later use, such as in hot pot or stir-fries.

Fried Pasta with Vegetarian Lotus Root Balls

I grew up in southern China, where lotus roots are a local specialty, so they often appear in various forms on my dining table. Lotus roots come in different varieties, some are powdery and sticky, while others are crisp and refreshing. I prefer using the powdery lotus roots to make a large batch of lotus root balls at once. Whether I put them in soup, add them to spaghetti, plant-based bowls, or even enjoy them on their own as a snack, they make for a delightful choice.

Ingredients

A

- 14 oz lotus roots
- 3½ oz low gluten flour
- 3½ oz firm tofu
- ¼ tsp salt
- 1 Tbsp light soy sauce
- 1 Tbsp dark soy sauce
- 1 c vegetable oil

B

- 2 oz butterfly-shaped pasta
- ¼ oz sweet peas
- ¼ oz kale
- ¼ tsp salt
- 1 Tbsp canola oil
- 1 Tbsp light soy sauce
- 1 qt water

C

- ¼ oz purple cabbage
- ¼ oz cashews
- ¼ oz almonds
- dash of seaweed seasoning

Instructions

❶ Use set A to make the lotus root balls. Peel the lotus roots, cut them into chunks, and chop or use a blender to crush them, retaining some coarse texture of the lotus root. Sprinkle with a bit of salt and let it sit for 15 minutes to release more lotus root juice, which will be used later. Place the lotus root mixture in cheesecloth and squeeze out as much liquid as possible. Crumble the firm tofu and squeeze out any excess moisture using cheesecloth as well. Mix the lotus root mixture with low gluten flour, crumbled tofu, salt, light soy sauce, and dark soy sauce. Ensure all ingredients are well combined. Depending on the consistency after mixing, if it's too dry, add some of the lotus root juice reserved from earlier to moisten the mixture. Shape the mixture into evenly sized balls. Heat oil in a pan, then reduce the heat to low. Carefully place the lotus root balls into the hot oil and fry until golden and crispy.

❷ Use set B to make the stir-fried pasta. Cook the pasta in a pot of boiling water for about 15 minutes until it is cooked through. In a separate frying pan, heat canola oil. Add salt, sweet peas, cooked pasta, and light soy sauce in turn, and stir-fry for 5 minutes. Just before removing from the heat, mix in the kale.

❸ For set C, after washing the purple cabbage, shred it into thin strips. Assemble all the ingredients and serve.

Plant-Based Bowl with Arrowhead and Lotus Root Balls

The arrowhead is a Chinese specialty vegetable, known as one of the "eight water immortals," and is also highly valued for its medicinal properties as an ingredient. Arrowhead has a velvety texture, with an initial bitter taste followed by sweetness, which also offers a refreshing aroma. Therefore, pairing them with deep-fried lotus root balls in a braised dish helps to balance out the greasiness effectively.

Ingredients

A

- 3 arrowheads
- 2 lotus root balls
- 1 broccoli floret
- 1 Tbsp vegetable oil
- 1 tsp coconut palm sugar
- 1 tsp soy sauce
- 1 tsp vegetarian oyster sauce
- ⅙ oz salt
- ½ c water

B

- 1½ oz tricolor brown rice with red beans
- 1 tsp seaweed seasoning
- 1 tsp kale

Instructions

❶ For set A, clean and peel the arrowheads. Cut them in half and place them in a bowl. Add enough salted water to cover the arrowheads and let them soak for 10 minutes. Afterward, rinse them thoroughly and drain. Next, blanch the arrowheads in boiling water to remove any bitterness. Heat oil in a pot, add the lotus root balls, blanched arrowheads, and broccoli, stir-fry. Then, add an appropriate amount of water, followed by coconut palm sugar, soy sauce, and vegetarian oyster sauce for seasoning. Continue frying until the sauce reduces.

❷ For set B, soak the tricolor brown rice and red beans for about 4 to 8 hours beforehand. Add water 1 cm above the level of the rice and boil them in a pot for approximately 20 minutes until done, or cook them with a rice cooker using its brown rice setting (the tricolor brown rice and red beans can be replaced with regular rice or other staples). After washing the kale, shake off excess water. Combine all the ingredients together, then sprinkle with some seaweed seasoning.

Fried Tofu Pouches with Fish Mint

Fish mint's scientific name is "Houttuynia cordata." Its acceptance varies greatly among people from different regions due to its unique smell. Growing up in the southwestern region of China, I have always used fish mint as a seasoning in various dishes. This snack is inspired by roadside stalls I encountered while traveling. The firm tofu, with its crispy exterior and a burst of flavor inside, wraps around the fresh, tangy, spicy fish mint. It's a delightful treat, and you can easily devour a large bowl in no time.

Ingredients
(for 5 tofu pouches)

A

- 14 oz firm tofu
- 1 c vegetable oil

B

- 7 oz fish mint
- 1 Tbsp soy sauce
- 2 tsp brown rice vinegar
- 2 Tbsp chili oil
- 1 tsp maple syrup
- ¼ tsp salt

Instructions

❶ Use set A to fry the firm tofu. Drain excess water from the tofu and cut it into large pieces. Steam it for 10 minutes, then allow it to cool. Pour an appropriate amount of oil into a pan and heat it up. When the oil starts to emit a slight wisp of smoke, reduce the heat to medium-low and carefully add the tofu to fry. After placing the tofu in the pan, avoid flipping it immediately to prevent breaking it. Let it fry for a while until the tofu expands and floats up. Then, flip it over and continue frying until it turns golden brown.

❷ Use set B to make the cold salad with fish mint. Wash the fish mint and chop it finely. In a small bowl, add chili oil, soy sauce, vinegar, maple syrup, and salt in order. Stir well to make the dressing, then mix it evenly with the chopped fish mint.

❸ After frying the tofu, tear open a hole in one side of the tofu pouch. Then, stuff it with the cold salad made from fish mint.

fish mint

Tips

A tip for frying tofu: firm tofu has less moisture and a firmer texture, making it easier to fry to a crisp. Steaming it first before frying helps remove the beany flavor and allows the tofu to become drier and puffier, resulting in a tough texture. When frying, using high oil temperature will quickly harden the outer surface, thus isolating the inside of the tofu, preventing it from absorbing too much oil.

The roots of fish mint have many fine hairs and need to be thoroughly cleaned.

Vegetable Bowl with Purple Carrot

Grown in the Yunnan Province in the southwest of China, purple carrots are the most suitable carrots for making salads. I first discovered that they came in this color on a trip to a farm, and I felt curious about its taste, so I pulled one from the ground and took it home. After cleaning and peeling it, I couldn't resist taking a bite of it raw—I was amazed to find that carrots could be so sweet and crunchy!

Ingredients

A

- 2 oz tricolor beans tempeh
- 1 Tbsp coconut oil

B

- 7 broccoli florets
- 2 white mushrooms
- 1 Tbsp vegetable oil

C

- ⅓ avocado
- 1 purple carrot
- ½ oz kale
- ¼ oz pecans
- 1 Tbsp vinaigrette (see page 24 for recipe)

Instructions

❶ For set A, slice the tempeh, grease a frying plan with the coconut oil, and sauté the tempeh until both sides turn brown and crisp.

❷ For set B, rinse the broccoli florets and white mushrooms, slice the mushrooms, grease with the vegetable oil, and roast in the oven at 180 ℃ for 10 minutes.

❸ For set C, peel and slice the avocado, cut the purple carrot into thin slices, and wash the kale and shake them dry.

❹ Assemble all the ingredients, add pecans and drizzle with vinaigrette.

Chapter Five
Green Leafy Vegetables

The affinity between the Chinese people and wild vegetables can be seen in the *Book of Songs* (*Shijing*). Someone has done a rough statistical analysis, revealing that among the 305 poems in the *Book of Songs*, there are mentions of edible wild vegetables in as many as 43 poems, encompassing 25 different types. Foraging wild vegetables has thus become a part of Chinese life. This chapter shares green leafy vegetables that are not limited to the common types found on the dining table. Instead, it explores the flavors of wild vegetables that grow naturally in the mountains, forests, and fields. Though they may seem inconspicuous, they are rich in nutrients and have therapeutic effects.

Water Shield and Tofu Soup

Water shield originated in China and belongs to the category of rare aquatic plants. It grows in clean water, and its tender shoots are covered with naturally occurring transparent jelly-like gel. Alongside water shield, water bamboo shoots, and perch, they are collectively known as the "three famous dishes of Jiangnan." Cooked together with smooth and tender tofu to make a thick soup, the texture is delicate, fresh, sweet, and delicious.

Ingredients

- 7 oz soft tofu
- 1 piece of button mushroom
- 1 piece of shiitake mushroom
- 1 oz water shield
- ¼ tsp salt
- 2 c pure vegetable broth
- dash of white sesame

Instructions

❶ Cut the soft tofu into chunks. Slice the button mushroom and shiitake mushroom. Rinse the water shield thoroughly with clean water. The vegetable broth can be made by simmering edible fungus and kombu in pure water for 20 to 30 minutes.

❷ In a soup pot, pour the vegetable broth. First, add the water shield and cook for 5 minutes. Then, sequentially add the button mushroom, shiitake mushroom, a little salt, and white sesame.

Bean Vermicelli with Red Amaranth

Tip

Choose red amaranth that are more tender for better tasting soup.

Red amaranth is commonly stir-fried or boiled into a soup. When cooked with bean vermicelli, the soft, smooth vermicelli and the richly flavored vegetables are fragrant and sweet in taste, and make for an unforgettable dish. During my childhood, every time I spot red amaranth in a meal at home, I'd fetch a big spoon to scoop the purplish-red broth that it produces over my rice. This would give me a bowl of rose-colored rice which absolutely whets my appetite!

Ingredients

- 2 oz red amaranth
- 3 oz wet bean vermicelli
- 1 Tbsp vegetable oil
- 3 c kombu broth (see page 25 for recipe)
- 2 tsp soy sauce
- ¼ tsp salt

Instructions

❶ Wash the red amaranth.

❷ Add the vegetable oil to a pot and stir-fry the red amaranth briefly before adding the kombu broth to cook for about 3 minutes.

❸ Add the bean vermicelli, followed by the salt and then the soy sauce, and cook for another 5 minutes or so.

Plant-Based Bowl with Chinese Broccoli

There is a Chinese poem describing Chinese broccoli as having the delicious taste of mushrooms and the sweet and refreshing taste of green leafy vegetables. Putting it in your mouth and chewing it, you can also feel its tenderness and crispness. This can be considered high praise for vegetables. So in this dish, I simply blanch the Chinese broccoli in boiling water to preserve its natural flavor as much as possible.

Ingredients

A

- 2 oz dried tofu
- ½ oz bean sprouts
- 2 seaweed sheets
- 1 oz brown rice
- ½ oz pinto beans
- 1 oz Chinese broccoli
- 1 walnut
- 1 Tbsp vegetable oil

B

- ½ oz minced garlic
- 1 Tbsp vegetable oil
- 1 tsp light soy sauce
- 1 tsp dark soy sauce
- 1 tsp maple syrup

Instructions

❶ For set A, stir-fry the dried tofu and Chinese broccoli separately in a pan brushed with oil until cooked. Blanch the bean sprouts in boiling water until tender. Roast the walnut in a pan for 5 minutes until fragrant and crispy.

❷ After washing the brown rice and pinto beans, soak them for about 4 to 8 hours beforehand. Add water 1 cm above the level of the rice, then boil it in a pot for approximately 20 minutes until done, or cook it with a rice cooker using its brown rice setting.

❸ Use set B to prepare the garlic-infused oil sauce. Heat a frying pan, add vegetable oil, and then fry the minced garlic until fragrant. In a small bowl, mix together light soy sauce, dark soy sauce, and maple syrup until well combined, then drizzle the hot garlic oil over the mixture.

❹ Combine all the ingredients in a bowl, and before consuming, drizzle with the garlic-infused oil sauce or add any pickles you like according to personal taste preferences.

Steamed Purslane with Flour

Purslane is a wild, delicious vegetable that grows tenaciously. It can be found everywhere, in cracks on the roadside, at the corners of walls, and beside fences. When you're cooking purslane in the height of summer, the rising steam from the uncovered steamer will release a faint aroma of the wild vegetable. Taking a bite while the vegetable is hot, its natural and original deliciousness will blossom on your tongue.

Ingredients

- 2 oz purslane
- ¼ tsp salt
- 1 Tbsp vegetable oil
- 2 tsp cornstarch
- 1 oz whole wheat flour

Instructions

❶ Wash the purslane thoroughly and shake off excess water. Pour vegetable oil over the purslane and mix well. Then, sprinkle with cornstarch and whole wheat flour, stirring evenly with chopsticks while sprinkling. The flour should thinly coat and evenly cover the purslane.

❷ Preheat the steamer by adding water and bringing it to a boil. Evenly spread the mixed purslane on the steamer tray. Steam for about 10 minutes.

Tip

Purslane can also be enjoyed as a cold salad. Here's how to prepare it: Wash the purslane thoroughly and shake off excess water. Blanch the purslane in boiling water until it is just cooked. To prepare the cold salad dressing, mix together sesame oil, brown rice vinegar, soy sauce, and chili powder in a small bowl. Drizzle this mixture over the blanched purslane. This makes for a refreshing appetizer perfect for summer.

Pumpkin Vines and Asparagus with Sesame Sauce

During the summer, the garden is abundant with a variety of vegetables and fruits, adorning the yard with vitality. Pumpkin vines also grow vigorously during this period, producing the most tender and delicious shoots. After harvesting, they are cleaned and blanched in boiling water before being tossed with cold salad dressing. With their bright green color and crispy yet tender texture, they offer a refreshing and slightly spicy taste, making them an excellent appetizer for summer.

Ingredients

A

- 3 oz pumpkin vines
- 4 to 5 asparagus spears
- moderate amount of water
- a pinch of salt

B

- 1 Tbsp light soy sauce
- 1 Tbsp dark soy sauce
- 1 Tbsp balsamic vinegar
- 1 Tbsp white sesame
- ¼ tsp salt
- 2 Tbsp vegetable oil
- 1 Tbsp chili powder

C

- 4 shiitake mushrooms
- 7 oz firm tofu
- 2 tsp soy sauce
- 1 oz whole wheat flour
- ¼ tsp salt

Instructions

❶ For set A, try to choose tender pumpkin vines. After washing, you can peel off the outer skin, but it is optional. In a pot, bring water to a boil with a pinch of salt. Blanch the pumpkin vines and asparagus spears in the boiling water for 1 minute, then remove and immediately soak them in cold water.

❷ Use set B to prepare the white sesame spicy and sour dressing. In a small bowl, combine the light soy sauce, dark soy sauce, balsamic vinegar, and salt. Heat the vegetable oil in a pan until hot, then turn off the heat. Add the white sesame seeds and chili powder to the hot oil, then pour the mixture into the small bowl and stir until well mixed.

❸ Use set C to prepare the shiitake mushroom tofu patties. Finely chop the shiitake mushrooms. Drain excess water from the firm tofu and crumble it. Mix together the crumbled tofu, chopped shiitake mushrooms, whole wheat flour, salt, and soy sauce until evenly mixed. Brush a layer of oil onto a pan and fry the mushroom tofu mixture into patties of the same size until both sides are golden and crispy.

❹ Assemble all the ingredients and serve.

Garland Chrysanthemum Salad Bowl

Garland chrysanthemum is commonly stir-fried or used in hot pots. Although it's not often seen in salads, this vegetable can actually be eaten raw. Pick the tenderer leaves, briefly soak them in water, and place them in the refrigerator to keep them fresh. Enjoy this simple salad under the sun in the warm months of March and April, when the spring flowers are blooming, and savor the sweet scent of the garland chrysanthemums.

Ingredients

A

- 1 oz garland chrysanthemum
- 1 fig
- 1 oz tricolor beans tempeh
- 2 tsp vegetable oil
- ½ oz chickpeas
- ¼ oz quinoa
- ½ avocado
- ½ tsp black and white sesame
- 2 longans
- ¼ oz pomegranate seeds
- ¼ tsp salt
- ¼ tsp cumin powder

B

- 2 tsp tangerine juice
- 2 tsp olive oil
- 2 tsp maple syrup
- ¼ tsp black pepper

Instructions

❶ For set A, wash the garland chrysanthemum and shake them dry. Cut the fig into small pieces. Soak the chickpeas 4 hours in advance before cooking them in a pressure cooker, then fry them in oil until crispy. Remove the chickpeas from the heat and sprinkle with salt and cumin powder for added flavor. Slice the tempeh and fry them in oil until both sides turn brown and crisp. Cook the quinoa in a pot for about 20 minutes.

❷ For set B, combine all the seasonings in a small bowl and mix well.

❸ Plate all the ingredients and serve.

Garland Chrysanthemum with Soy Milk Pot

Garland Chrysanthemum thrives in winter, and a common practice is to enjoy them in spicy hot pot broths. However, in this recipe, I've replaced the traditional broth with a rich and nutritious soy milk base. The fragrant and flavorful soy milk soup complements the fresh garland chrysanthemum perfectly. Gathering around the bubbling pot with family, enjoying this dish together, creates the perfect experience for winter days.

Ingredients

A

• 3 oz soybeans
• 1 qt water
• 1 Tbsp soy sauce
• ¼ tsp ginger paste
• 1 Tbsp miso paste
• 1 piece of dried kelp

B

• 1 oz garland chrysanthemum
• 6 pieces of bean curd roll
• ½ carrot

Instructions

❶ Use set A to make fresh soy milk. Soak the soybeans in water for 8 hours. After rinsing them thoroughly, put them into a soy milk maker along with clean water to make fresh soy milk. Alternatively, you can use unsweetened soy milk powder or directly purchase unsweetened soy milk. Soak the dried kelp in water in advance. In a soup pot, combine fresh soy milk, soaked kelp, soy sauce, ginger paste, and miso paste to make the soy milk soup base.

❷ For set B, wash the fresh garland chrysanthemum and shake off excess water. Cut the bean curd rolls into long strips of equal size. Roll up the garland chrysanthemum leaves and secure them with small toothpicks. Peel the carrot and cut it into long strips. Add the garland chrysanthemum and bean curd rolls to the soy milk soup base and cook for 5 minutes.

Fried Rice with Chinese Toon and Matsutake Mushroom

The Chinese toon tree is native to China. What people can eat are the tender shoots growing at the top of the trees. The fresher and tenderer the Chinese toon shoots are, the better they taste. Therefore, the timing and method of harvesting require a lot of experience. In spring, in order to obtain the fragrant and tender Chinese toon shoots, people hurry to the market early to buy them. As a result, Chinese toon shoots are often in high demand.

Ingredients

- 1 oz Chinese toon
- 2 oz brown rice
- 1 Tbsp soy sauce
- 1 Tbsp vegetable oil
- 1 oz carrot
- 1 oz yellow bell pepper
- 1 matsutake mushroom
- ¼ oz pistachios

Instructions

❶ After blanching the fresh Chinese toon until cooked, chop it finely. Dice the fresh matsutake mushroom, yellow bell pepper, and carrot and set aside.

❷ Soak the brown rice for about 4 to 8 hours beforehand. Add water 1 cm above the level of the rice and boil it in a pot for approximately 20 minutes until done, or cook it with a rice cooker using its brown rice setting. In a pot, add a little vegetable oil and heat it up. Then, add the diced matsutake mushroom and stir-fry until cooked. Next, add the diced carrot and Chinese toon, and finally add the brown rice. Drizzle with soy sauce, and stir-fry until well mixed. Finally, sprinkle with some pistachios.

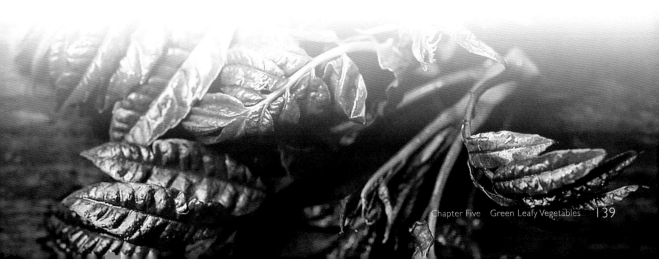

Kale Salad with Avocado Basil Dressing

Does your stomach feel heavy after the holidays? This dish can be considered a lifesaver after a big meal. The sweet and rich avocado sauce wrapped around the shredded kale and cabbage, mixed with the refreshing scent of basil and the coolness of peaches, makes you feel like your body is liberated from greasiness, filled with vitality to face new challenges.

Ingredients

A

- ½ oz kale
- ½ oz purple cabbage
- ½ oz yellow peach
- ¼ oz green lentils
- ½ oz tricolor quinoa
- ¼ avocado
- ½ tsp chia seeds
- ½ tsp hemp seeds

B

- ½ avocado
- 1 tsp basil
- 2 tsp lemon juice
- 2 tsp olive oil
- 2 tsp maple syrup

Instructions

❶ In set A, wash the kale thoroughly and shake off excess water. Shred the purple cabbage. Peel and slice the peach. Slice ¼ of the avocado into strips. Boil the green lentils in water for about 20 minutes until cooked. Also, cook the tricolor quinoa in water for approximately 20 minutes.

❷ Use set B to make the avocado basil dressing. Combine all ingredients in a food processor and blend into a thick sauce.

❸ Combine the ingredients from set A and arrange them on a plate. Sprinkle with chia seeds and hemp seeds, then drizzle with the avocado basil dressing and serve.

Mugwort Pancake

When I was a child, I loved going to the countryside, wandering around the mountains and fields, playing everywhere. In the fields and vegetable gardens, you could easily find mugwort. Mugwort has a unique fragrance. It is not only an herb, but it can also be used to make various delicacies, such as green rice balls, and this mugwort pancake, which has a faint medicinal fragrance.

Ingredients

A

- 1 oz wild mugwort
- ½ c plant-based milk
- 3 oz brown rice flour
- 1 Tbsp maple syrup
- ¼ tsp vanilla extract
- 1 Tbsp canola oil

B

- 4 pieces of banana
- 1 strawberry
- dash of white sesame
- ½ tsp vegetable oil

Instructions

❶ Use set A to make the mugwort pancake. Remove the leaves from the mugwort, wash them, and use a salad spinner to remove excess water. Blend the mugwort leaves and plant-based milk in a food processor to make a mugwort paste. In a mixing bowl, add brown rice flour, vanilla extract, and maple syrup, and mix well. Then add the mugwort paste to the mixture and stir until well combined, forming a dough-like consistency that is neither too dry nor too runny. Brush a layer of canola oil on a non-stick pan and cook the pancakes over low heat until both sides are crispy and brown.

❷ For set B, peel the banana and cut it into four pieces. Brush a layer of oil on a flat-bottomed pan, using minimal oil, or you can skip the oil altogether and lightly grill the banana pieces. Wash the strawberry and cut it in half. Combine the ingredients together, then sprinkle some white sesame on top.

Shepherd's Purse Balls

Shepherd's purse is one of the most common tastes of spring. It is popular with people in both northern and southern China, who eagerly indulge in its fresh flavor during the springtime. Shepherd's purse has a refreshing aroma and a tender, crisp texture. Clean and chop it finely, and it can be used for cold salads, soups, dumplings, or meatballs. Some say, "A spring without eating shepherd's purse is a soulless spring." This shows that shepherd's purse is one of the flavors that best represents spring for the Chinese people.

Ingredients

- 3 oz firm tofu
- 1 oz shepherd's purse
- 2 shiitake mushrooms
- 1 oz low gluten flour
- ¼ oz breadcrumbs
- ½ c vegetable oil

Instructions

❶ Remove excess moisture from the firm tofu, then crumble it. Squeeze out the excess water using cheesecloth. Wash the shiitake mushrooms and shepherd's purse, then chop them finely into small pieces.

❷ In a large bowl, combine the crumbled firm tofu, chopped shiitake mushrooms, chopped shepherd's purse, and low gluten flour. Knead the mixture into a dry dough. Then, roll the dough into evenly sized balls and coat them with breadcrumbs.

❸ Pour vegetable oil into a small pot and heat it over high heat until hot. Reduce the heat to low and carefully add the shepherd's purse balls into the hot oil. Fry them until they are golden brown and crispy on the outside. Depending on personal preference, you can enhance the flavor by adding chili powder or tomato sauce.

❹ Arrange the shepherd's purse balls on a serving plate. For decoration, you can use small flowers such as daisies to enhance the visual appeal.

Perilla Tomato Avocado

Perilla, native to China, is commonly used as a spice. In this dish, the unique flavor of perilla enhances the taste level. With each bite, there's a stunning sensation that surpasses the natural flavors of the ingredients.

Ingredients

A

- 1 avocado
- 1 tomato
- ¼ oz fresh perilla leaves

B

- 1 tsp perilla oil
- 1 tsp maple syrup
- 1 tsp soy sauce
- 1 tsp lemon juice
- ½ tsp hemp seeds

Instructions

❶ For ingredients A, peel and pit the avocado, then cut it in half. Wash the tomato and cut it into chunks. After washing the perilla leaves, shake off excess water, and you can cut them into thin strips.

❷ For ingredients B, mix the perilla oil, maple syrup, soy sauce, and lemon juice in a small bowl until well mixed. Drizzle this mixture over the avocado, and finally, sprinkle with hemp seeds.

Daylily with Mushroom and Tomato

Tips

Fresh daylily contains colchicine, which itself is non-toxic. However, when ingested, it can be oxidized in the body and cause strong irritation to the gastrointestinal and respiratory systems. So before consumption, it is essential to blanch the daylily in boiling water at a temperature of 60 ℃ . This can remove the toxins. It should also be soaked for 2 hours to ensure safe consumption.

Dried daylily does not contain toxins and can be consumed safely. Before consumption, it should be soaked in clean water for 1 to 2 hours to rehydrate.

Daylily sprouts in spring, its leaves resembling orchids, lush and green. In summer, they blossom into patches, with red and yellow flowers dancing in the wind like butterflies. By autumn, people harvest them for cooking. Fresh daylily has thick and succulent stems, a fragrant floral taste, and is also known for its medicinal properties to calm the mind and clear heat.

Ingredients

- 7 oz fresh daylily
- 5 oz cherry tomatoes
- 2 fresh shiitake mushrooms
- 1 Tbsp vegetable oil
- 1 tsp mushroom powder
- 1 Tbsp soy sauce
- 1 tsp white sesame
- ½ tsp dried basil leaves
- ¼ tsp salt

Instructions

❶ After washing the daylily, blanch it in boiling water for about 3 to 5 minutes. Then, soak it in clean water for 2 to 3 hours.

❷ Cut a cross on the cherry tomatoes, blanch them in boiling water briefly, then peel off the skin and dice them. Dice the shiitake mushrooms as well.

❸ In a pan, heat oil and add the diced shiitake mushrooms and diced tomatoes. Stir-fry briefly, then add salt, white sesame seeds, mushroom powder, and soy sauce in order. Once cooked, pour this mixture over the blanched daylily. Finally, garnish with dried basil leaves. Mix well and serve.

Chapter Six
Fresh Fruits

Most fruits are harvested in the summer and autumn seasons. During this time, wandering through the orchards in the countryside as the sun rises, the garden filled with fruits hanging from the branches is illuminated by the gentle sunlight. Kiwi, plums, peaches, chestnuts, pears ... The colorful orchard resembles a palette of nature, bringing joy to the heart and inspiring me with many culinary ideas.

To many, fruits might seem difficult to incorporate into cooking beyond just eating them raw. However, in whole plant-based bowls, fruits can also play a significant role as key ingredients. In salads, we can directly experience their natural flavors. In fruit wines, we can savor the rich aroma of different fruits. When made into snacks, they can tantalize the taste buds and leave us craving for more.

Veggie Bowl with Blood Orange and Pumpkin

The flesh of blood oranges is as colorful and vibrant as its name suggests. Every time I use it in cooking, I feel like the dish gains a tropical island vibe. It has a rich texture, sweet taste, and a hint of rose fragrance with a slight tanginess. Adding it to salads not only enhances the color palette but also brings a refreshing citrus aroma.

Ingredients

A

- ½ baby pumpkin
- 2 tsp olive oil
- ¼ tsp salt
- 1 Tbsp cornstarch
- 1 oz tricolor brown rice

B

- 1 Tbsp white sesame
- ½ oz chickpeas
- 1 tsp oil
- ¼ tsp salt

C

- 1 blood orange
- ½ oz endives
- ½ oz purple cabbage
- ¼ oz pumpkin seeds
- 1 Tbsp sesame cheese sauce (see page 24 for recipe)

Instructions

❶ For set A, cut the baby pumpkin into chunks, then mix it with a little olive oil, salt, and cornstarch. Cook it in an air fryer or oven for 15 minutes. Soak the tricolor brown rice for about 4 to 8 hours beforehand. Add water 1 cm above the level of the rice, then boil it in a pot for approximately 20 minutes until done, or cook it with a rice cooker using its brown rice setting.

❷ Use set B to make crispy chickpeas. Soak the chickpeas for 4 hours in advance, then cook them until tender. Drain the excess water and toss them with oil and salt until well mixed. Place them in the oven and bake for 10 to 15 minutes.

❸ For set C, peel the blood orange and slice it into rounds. Wash and dry the endives and purple cabbage. Slice the purple cabbage into fine strips.

❹ Combine all the ingredients together, sprinkle with pumpkin seeds, and drizzle with sauce to serve.

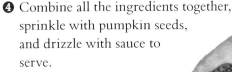

Warm Salad with Baked Orange

Tip

For this dish, choose larger navel oranges, not only are they succulent, but they don't spread as easily during baking.

Since I was young, I've always been prone to coughing when the seasons change. At these times, my family would take an orange, poke a few holes in it, and bake it over the fire. After eating two baked oranges, the cough magically stopped, and the whole house would be filled with the fragrance of oranges.

Ingredients

A

- 1 navel orange
- 1 oz tricolor quinoa
- 1 oz lentils
- ⅕ avocado
- ½ oz endives
- 1 strawberry
- 1 oz plant-based protein crumbles
- ⅕ oz pumpkin seeds
- a pinch of salt

B

- 1 Tbsp ginger oil
- 1 Tbsp apple cider vinegar
- 1 Tbsp maple syrup
- ¼ tsp sea salt

Instructions

❶ For set A, after peeling the navel orange, slice it evenly into thick rounds and place them on a baking tray. Bake them at medium heat for about 5 minutes. Soak the tricolor quinoa and lentils for 10 minutes, then steam them until cooked in a steamer pot. Dice the avocado and strawberry into small pieces. Wash the endives and shake off water. Soak the plant-based protein crumbles for 20 minutes, squeeze out the excess water, add a pinch of salt, then place them on a baking tray and bake for 10 minutes.

❷ Use set B to make the ginger vinaigrette. Mix the ginger oil, apple cider vinegar, maple syrup, and sea salt in a small bowl until well combined.

❸ Arrange all the ingredients on a plate, sprinkle with pumpkin seeds, and drizzle with the ginger vinaigrette.

Cucumber Berry Bowl

Eating a chilled cucumber in the summer makes one realize that "coolness" can not only describe the weather, but also a scent or flavor. Chewing on a cucumber with its skin intact, the astringency and thickness of the skin mingle with the sweetness and tenderness of the flesh, filling the mouth with the fragrance of green grass.

Ingredients

- 4 strawberries
- 1 cucumber
- 6 mulberries
- 2 pecans
- ¼ oz lettuce
- ¼ oz kale
- 1 Tbsp vinaigrette (see page 24 for recipe)

Instructions

❶ Wash the strawberries, cucumber, mulberries, kale, and lettuce, then shake off excess water.

❷ Cut the strawberries in half. Slice the cucumber into thin strips, then roll them up.

❸ Assemble all the ingredients together and drizzle with vinaigrette to serve.

Wild Pear Salad

There are many varieties of pears, some with soft and delicate flesh, while others have firm and crunchy texture with graininess. Every autumn, I go to the mountains to pick a few wild pears from the trees. The flesh of wild pears is crisp and sweet, with abundant juice and small cores. Eating thinly sliced pears combined with seasonal ingredients can moisten the lungs and relieve dryness in autumn.

Ingredients

A

- 1 wild pear
- 1 fig
- 1 oz kale
- ½ small cucumber
- 1 oz tricolor quinoa
- ½ avocado

B

- 2 white passion fruits
- 2 tsp maple syrup
- 2 tsp apple cider vinegar
- 2 tsp olive oil

Instructions

❶ For set A, wash the wild pear and fig. Slice them. Wash the kale, shake off water, and break it into small florets, then peel and slice the cucumber into strips. Remove the shell and cut the avocado in half. Wash the tricolor quinoa and cook it in water for about 20 minutes.

❷ For set B, put the passion fruits, maple syrup, apple cider vinegar, and olive oil into a small bowl, then mix them evenly.

❸ Assemble all the ingredients and serve.

Plum Wine

Plums are the most suitable fruit for making wine. They have a balanced sweetness and acidity, fragrant skin, and vibrant color, which result in a refreshing taste, pleasant acidity, and a blush pink color in the wine.

Ingredients

- 10 to 11 plums
- 1 oz yellow rock sugar
- 2 c low-alcohol content liquor

Instructions

❶ Wash the plums thoroughly, remove the stems, and allow the skins to air dry to remove excess moisture.

❷ For soaking wine, choose a glass jar of around 1 qt in size. After washing it thoroughly, disinfect it to ensure there is no water or oil residue inside the container.

❸ In the glass jar, layer the yellow rock sugar and plums alternately, repeating the process until all the ingredients are stacked.

❹ Finally, add the low-alcohol content liquor, seal the jar tightly, and store it in a cool, dry place. Let it steep for at least six months for better flavor.

Chia Seeds Lychee Cup

Lychees ripen from early to mid-summer, with bright red shells and translucent, sweet, and tender flesh. As a delicate fruit, Chinese poets have described it as follows, "Color changes in a day, fragrance changes in two days, taste changes in three days, and by the fourth day, color, fragrance, and taste are all gone." Since ancient times, countless literati, merchants, and nobles have tried various methods to preserve lychees, leading to the proliferation of numerous stories about lychees.

Ingredients

A

- 5 lychees
- 3 to 4 mint leaves

B

- ¼ c chia seeds
- ½ c almond milk
- ½ c maple syrup

Instructions

❶ For set A, peel and deseed the lychees, and wash the mint leaves.

❷ For set B, pour almond milk into a glass bowl, then add maple syrup and chia seeds. Stir and mix well, then refrigerate for 2 hours.

❸ After cleaning the glass jar, pour in the chilled chia seed almond milk pudding. Then add the peeled lychee flesh and garnish with mint leaves.

Plant-Based Cheese Bowl with Wax Apple

Wax apples grow in southern China and are a fruit with extremely high water content. They are also considered excellent for cooling and relieving heat. Since wax apples themselves don't have a strong distinctive flavor, I pair them with homemade plant-based cheese. Combining juicy and light fruit with rich and creamy cheese results in a perfect combination of vitamins and protein.

Ingredients

A

- 2 wax apples
- ½ oz kale
- ½ oz rocket leaves
- ¼ oz pumpkin seeds
- 3 almonds
- 1 Tbsp maple syrup

B

- ½ oz chickpeas
- 1 tsp oil
- ¼ tsp salt

C

- 3 oz firm tofu
- 1 Tbsp olive oil
- 2 tsp lemon juice
- 2 tsp apple cider vinegar
- 1 Tbsp miso
- ½ tsp salt
- 1 Tbsp dried basil
- 2 tsp agar powder
- ⅛ c water

Instructions

❶ For set A, wash the wax apples and slice them. Wash the kale and rocket leaves, then shake off water.

❷ Use set B to make crispy chickpeas. Soak the chickpeas for 4 hours in advance, then cook them until tender. Drain the excess water and toss them with oil and salt until well mixed. Place them in the oven and bake for 10 to 15 minutes.

❸ Use set C to make plant-based cheese. Wrap the firm tofu in cheesecloth and place a weighted object on top to remove excess moisture. Blend the firm tofu, olive oil, lemon juice, apple cider vinegar, miso, and salt in a food processor until smooth. Then add dried basil and blend again until evenly mixed. After thoroughly mixing agar powder and water, heat the mixture until it forms agar gel, which acts as a setting agent for the cheese. Refrigerate overnight, then cut into small pieces before serving.

❹ Combine all the ingredients, sprinkle with pumpkin seeds and almonds, and drizzle with maple syrup as desired to serve.

Grape Vegetable Bowl

Grapes are plentifully produced in Xinjiang, China, and harvested during the summer and autumn seasons. Clusters of grapes hang heavily from the vines in a variety of colors. There are so many varieties that one can't possibly try them all. They're used to make wine, grape jam, and salads. Different grape varieties present different flavors.

Ingredients

- 8 green grapes
- 14 blueberries
- ½ avocado
- 1 fig
- 2 to 3 kale leaves
- ⅓ oz pumpkin seeds
- ½ tsp hemp seeds
- 7 almonds
- 2 Tbsp vinaigrette (see page 24 for recipe)

Instructions

❶ Wash the green grapes, blueberries, kale leaves, fig and shake off water.

❷ Cut the avocado in half. Cut the fig into chunks. Choose raw pumpkin seeds and almonds.

❸ Combine all the ingredients together. Sprinkle some hemp seeds on top and drizzle with vinaigrette to serve.

Kiwi Salad

Kiwi originated in China and has a sweet and sour taste. It is acclaimed as the "king of vitamin C" and can be used to make jam, juice, and salads with other fruits and vegetables. It only takes ten minutes to make the kiwi salad. Refreshing and delicious, kiwi is a healthy superfood.

Ingredients

A

- 1 kiwi
- 2 oz wheatgrass
- 2 tsp sunflower seeds
- 2 oz cucumber
- ½ mango
- ½ oz red kidney beans
- ¼ oz pumpkin seeds
- 10 blueberries
- ¼ tsp chia seeds

B

- 1 Tbsp olive oil
- 1 Tbsp lemon juice
- 1 Tbsp maple syrup

Instructions

❶ For set A, soak the red kidney beans in water for 4 hours, then rinse them thoroughly and cook until tender. Wash the kiwi, peel it, and slice it into round shapes. Wash the wheatgrass and shake off water. Wash and dry the cucumber, and slice it into long strips. Wash the blueberries and cut them in half. Peel the mango, cut it in half, then slice it thinly. Roll each slice into a petal shape.

❷ Use set B to prepare the sauce. Mix olive oil, lemon juice, and maple syrup in a clean glass jar, cover it, and shake well to combine.

❸ Assemble all the ingredients in set A and drizzle with the sauce in set B to serve.

Perilla Peach Ginger

Tip

You can adjust the amount of rock sugar and vinegar according to your taste preference. Choose crisp peaches for the best flavor.

This is a specialty snack found in the streets and alleys of Hunan Province in central China. This refreshing and delicious dessert has a long history and places great importance on its ingredients. Crisp peaches, tender young ginger, and perilla leaves found in the mountains and plains are all summer ingredients, and each one is indispensable. After being pickled in glass jars and refrigerated, they become a taste exclusive to summer days.

Ingredients

- 3 peaches
- 3 oz young ginger
- 2 oz perilla leaves
- 2 oz yellow rock sugar
- 1 c purified water
- ¼ c brown rice vinegar

Instructions

❶ Wash the peaches with salt, then slice them thinly. Peel the young ginger and slice it thinly. Wash the perilla leaves, remove the stems, and finely chop the larger leaves.

❷ Wash the glass jar thoroughly and sterilize it either by using boiling water or a steamer.

❸ Add purified water, yellow rock sugar, and brown rice vinegar to the glass jar. Then, add the sliced peaches, young ginger, and perilla leaves into the glass jar and seal it tightly.

❹ Place it in the refrigerator and let it chill overnight before serving.

Roasted Chestnuts in Sugar

In the autumn and winter seasons, there are two unforgettable snacks found in the streets and alleys of China. The first one is the roasted sweet potato mentioned earlier, and the second one is roasted chestnuts. Chestnuts are stirred and roasted in a large pot, emitting crackling sounds. Their shells are coated with glistening syrup. When you peel the chestnuts, its fragrance, combined with caramelized sugar, wafts into the nose, making one's mouth water.

Ingredient

- 16 oz chestnuts
- 2 oz coconut sugar
- 3 Tbsp coconut oil

Instructions

❶ Wash the fresh chestnuts, then blanch them in boiling water for a moment. Use a knife to make a cross-shaped incision on each chestnut to facilitate peeling after roasting.

❷ After preparing the chestnuts, sprinkle some coconut sugar on them and brush them with a layer of coconut oil. Place them in the oven at 180 ℃ and roast for about 20 minutes.

Chestnut and Preserved Vegetable Rice Ball

Chestnuts are a delightful surprise you may find during autumn mountain hikes. As the wind blows, a few ripe chestnuts fall from the chestnut trees, and picking chestnuts becomes the most joyful activity. Adding chestnuts directly into whole grains and cooking them together creates a fragrant and hearty pot of food. If there's leftover, you can also knead them into various rice balls, making it convenient for picnics on the go.

dry preserved vegetable

Ingredients

A

- 2 oz chestnut kernels (weight after peeling)
- 3 dried flower mushrooms
- ¼ oz dry preserved vegetable
- 1 tsp soy sauce
- 1 Tbsp vegetable oil

B

- 3 oz tricolor brown rice

C

- ½ oz cauliflower
- ¼ avocado
- ¼ oz kale
- 5 to 6 almonds
- ½ tsp pumpkin seeds
- ½ tsp hemp seeds

Instructions

❶ For set A, fresh chestnuts should be washed and boiled until cooked. Then, peel them and set them aside. For dried flower mushrooms and the dry preserved vegetable, soak them in clean water for 3 to 4 hours beforehand. After soaking, dice the mushrooms and drain the preserved vegetable. Heat vegetable oil in a pan, add diced flower mushrooms and stir-fry until fragrant. Then, add the drained preserved vegetable and stir-fry until fragrant. Finally, add soy sauce and mix well.

❷ For set B, soak the tricolor brown rice for 4 to 8 hours beforehand. Add water 1 cm above the level of the rice, then boil it in a pot for approximately 20 minutes until done, or cook it with a rice cooker using its brown rice setting. Mix the sautéed diced flower mushrooms and preserved vegetable with the cooked chestnut kernels and tricolor brown rice. Shape the mixture into triangular rice balls.

❸ Wash the kale leaves and shake off water. Peel the avocado and cut it into chunks. Assemble all the ingredients and serve.

Sugar Coated Hawthorn with Sesame

Hawthorn fruit is native to China and grows in the northern regions. People have always liked these bright red and festive fruits. Due to their tart taste, they are often combined with sugar to make "sugar-coated haws." This sesame sugar hawthorn dish has a roasted sesame aroma and a crispy sugar coating, complemented by the sweet and tart flavor of hawthorn. It is especially suitable as an appetizing snack.

Ingredients

- 7 oz fresh hawthorn fruits
- 2 oz rock sugar
- ½ oz white sesame

Instructions

❶ Wash the fresh hawthorn fruits with salt.

❷ In a saucepan, add a little water just enough to cover the hawthorn fruits and rock sugar. Cook for about 5 minutes. Then, transfer them to a frying pan or oven. Fry at 150 ℃ for 15 minutes.

❸ Before serving, coat the hawthorn fruits with white sesame seeds. Use toothpicks to skewer them.

Dried Prunes and Apricots

Fresh prunes and apricots grow in the mountains, and after pickling and natural air drying, they can become long-lasting snacks. My memories of dried fruits stem from the experience of making them with my grandmother. This seemingly simple process requires long-term experience to produce a unique flavor. Even now, I find it very difficult to replicate the taste of dried fruits made by my grandmother. It is a flavor that belongs exclusively to her.

Ingredients

- 1 oz fresh prunes
- 1 oz fresh apricots

Instructions

Cut the fresh prunes and apricots in half, remove the pits, and sun-dry them to semi-dry or fully dry according to your preferred texture. Seal them in a glass jar for storage and try to consume them within one month. (Picture on the facing page is dried apricots, below is dried prunes.)

Hawthorn and Lotus Root Slices

When you don't have much appetite, you can try using hawthorn fruits in your cooking. Stir-fry it with thinly sliced crispy lotus root. The sourness of hawthorn fruits combined with the crispiness of lotus root will greatly increase your appetite.

Ingredients

- 2 oz fresh hawthorn fruits
- 3 oz lotus root
- ½ tsp sugar
- ¼ tsp vinegar
- a pinch of salt
- 1 Tbsp vegetable oil

Instructions

❶ Scrub the hawthorn fruits with salt until clean, then cut it into chunks. Peel the lotus root and slice it thinly.

❷ In a frying pan, add vegetable oil. Stir-fry the fresh hawthorn fruits, then add the lotus root slices. Season with sugar, vinegar, and salt. Stir-fry for 3 to 5 minutes, and it's ready to serve.

Fig Veggie Bowl

Figs have a sweet and sticky texture. They have high sugar content but low calories, and they are also rich in calcium, potassium, and selenium, which can enhance the body's antioxidant and anti-aging abilities. Before cutting open figs for consumption, remember to gently flatten them to ensure even distribution of sugar.

Ingredients

A

- 1 fig
- 2 prunes
- ½ oz lettuce
- ½ oz kale
- 1 cucumber
- 1 pecan
- ¼ oz pumpkin seeds

B

- 2 tsp perilla oil
- 2 tsp apple cider vinegar
- 2 tsp maple syrup

Instructions

❶ For set A, wash the fig and cut it into round slices. Wash the prunes and cut them in half. After washing the lettuce and kale, shake off excess water. Slice the cucumber into small rounds.

❷ For set B, put the perilla oil, apple cider vinegar, and maple syrup in a small bowl and mix well.

❸ Combine all the ingredients and drizzle the perilla oil vinegar mixture on top to serve.

Waxberry Wine

Waxberry wine is sour, sweet, and fragrant. When selecting seasonal waxberries, choose those about the size of ping-pong balls to soak in the wine. When the bottle is opened, the aroma of waxberry blends with the alcohol, hitting you instantly. With each sip, the wine's flavor is rich but not overpowering, accompanied by the lingering sweetness of waxberry. It tempts me to indulge in a few more glasses.

Ingredients

- 11 to 12 waxberries
- 6 oz yellow rock sugar
- 2 c low-alcohol content liquor

Instructions

❶ Soak the fresh waxberries in salted water for 15 minutes, then rinse them thoroughly and drain the water. Let them air dry.

❷ For soaking the wine, choose a glass jar of around 1 qt in size. After washing it thoroughly, sterilize it to ensure there's no water or oil residue inside the container.

❸ Layer the glass jar with alternating layers of rock sugar and waxberries. Repeat this process until the jar is filled.

❹ Finally, pour the low-alcohol content liquor into the jar. Seal the jar tightly and store it in a cool and dry place for at least six months. The longer it sits, the better the flavor.

Waxberry Lemon Drink

As an authentic Chinese fruit, waxberry is not only delicious eaten fresh, but also great when preserved or candied. This homemade waxberry drink is a perfect complement to hotpot. One sip may be hot and spicy, while the next is refreshing and cool. It provides relief from the spiciness while keeping you refreshed.

Ingredients

- 1½ lb waxberries
- 3 oz yellow rock sugar
- ½ lemon
- 4 c water
- dash of mint leaves

Instructions

❶ Soak the waxberries in salted water for 15 minutes, then rinse them thoroughly and drain the water. Slice the lemon.

❷ In a pot, add the water, then add the waxberries, rock sugar, and lemon slices in order. Bring to a boil over high heat, then reduce the heat to low and simmer for 30 minutes. Strain out the waxberry juice.

❸ After straining the waxberry juice, pour it into a sealed glass jar and refrigerate for 2 hours. Then, pour it into a glass, add the previously cooked waxberries and fresh lemon slices, and garnish with mint leaves and serve.

Waxberry Ice Jelly

Tip

The jelly tastes even better after chilling. When serving, feel free to add your favorite ingredients such as fruits and nuts.

During the scorching summer days, having a bowl of fruit jelly feels like hitting the pause button on the endless waves of heat, dispersing the sultry summer air. The deep purple waxberry juice permeates every translucent bubble of the jelly, along with your favorite toppings, making it a simple yet satisfying cool treat.

Ingredients
(for 3 servings)

A

- 1½ lb waxberries
- 2 oz maple syrup
- 4 c water
- ½ lemon

B

- 3 c waxberry juice
- 3 Tbsp agar powder
- ½ oz raisins
- ½ tsp hemp seeds

Instructions

❶ Use set A to make waxberry juice. Slice the lemon. Soak the waxberries in salted water for 15 minutes, then rinse them thoroughly and drain. In a pot, add water, then add the waxberries, maple syrup, and lemon slices in turn. Bring to a boil over high heat, then reduce the heat to low and simmer for 30 minutes. Strain out the waxberry juice and serve.

❷ Use set B to make waxberry jelly. Bring the waxberry juice to a boil in a pot. Then, add the agar powder and stir thoroughly until well mixed. Turn off the heat. Allow the mixture to cool and set at room temperature, then refrigerate for 2 hours. Add the raisins and hemp seeds before serving.

Chapter Seven
Mushrooms

The ingredient that best represents the taste of the wilderness in a plant-based diet is undoubtedly mushrooms. As the seasons transition from summer to autumn, after a refreshing autumn rain, mushrooms emerge from the ground like elves. They gather strength from winter to summer, carrying with them a longing for autumn, providing people wandering through the mountains and forests with a profound sense of surprise bestowed by nature. Mushrooms are delicious and nutritious, often referred to as delicacies from the mountains. In whole plant-based cuisine, using mushrooms as the main ingredient adds a natural and primitive charm, bringing forth the authentic taste of the wilderness.

Shiitake Mushroom Pancakes

Shiitake mushrooms can be considered one of the most common mushroom varieties on Chinese dining tables. They are versatile ingredients, whether used as a side dish in soups, stir-fries, or incorporated into main dishes with other vegetables. You can always taste the tender texture and unique aroma of shiitake mushrooms in the dishes.

Ingredients

A

- ½ oz kale
- 2 oz carrots
- 2 shiitake mushrooms
- 2 oz whole wheat flour
- 3 oz water
- 1 Tbsp vegetable oil

B

- 2 tsp vinaigrette (see page 24 for recipe)
- 1 fig
- ¼ oz endives
- ¼ oz kale
- ¼ oz pumpkin seeds
- 3 pieces of apple
- ¼ oz cooked kidney beans
- 2 tsp sesame paste
- ½ Tbsp roasted seaweed flakes

Instructions

❶ Use set A to make the vegetable pancake batter. Wash the kale and shake off excess water, then cut it into thin shreds. Peel and dice the carrots. Dice the shiitake mushrooms. Add them to the whole wheat flour and water and mix well.

❷ Heat vegetable oil in a pan over medium heat. Pour the whipped vegetable pancake batter into the pan and cook until golden brown on both sides, flipping as needed. Cut the pancake into several pieces.

❸ For set B, cut the fig into chunks. Pour the vinaigrette dressing into a bowl with the various fruits and vegetables, then mix well to make a salad.

❹ Place the shiitake mushroom pancake pieces on top of the salad. Drizzle sesame paste over the pancake, then sprinkle with roasted seaweed flakes.

Roasted Seaweed Buckwheat Noodles with Morel Mushrooms

Morel mushrooms are one of the mushroom varieties suitable for making soup. Due to the numerous pores on their surface, they can absorb the flavors of any ingredients and seasonings. The seaweed and morel mushrooms, soaked in soup, burst with flavor on the palate, providing a two-fold fresh and fragrant experience.

Ingredients

- ½ oz seaweed
- 1 Tbsp grape seed oil
- 1 dried morel mushroom
- 1 piece of dried bean curd stick
- 2 broccolini
- ¼ oz sweet peas
- 1½ c pure vegetable broth (see page 25 for recipe)
- 1 oz buckwheat noodles
- 1 Tbsp soy sauce
- ¼ tsp salt

Instructions

❶ Start by roasting the seaweed. Heat grape seed oil in a pan, then add the seaweed. Roast over low heat for 8 to 10 minutes.

❷ Soak the dried morel mushroom to rehydrate. Cook the buckwheat noodles in boiling water until done. While cooking the noodles, you can also blanch the broccolini, dried bean curd stick, sweet peas, and morel mushroom together in the pot.

❸ In a bowl, add the pure vegetable broth. Season with soy sauce and salt.

❹ Finally, add the cooked buckwheat noodles to the seasoned pure vegetable broth. Assemble all the ingredients and serve.

Radish Soup with Morel Mushroom

This is a very quick winter hot soup recipe that doesn't require overly complex ingredients. It can also be used as a broth for other dishes. On cold winter days, take a few minutes to prepare yourself a hot soup. One sip will warm you up from head to toe.

Ingredients

- 3 chunks of white radishes
- 2 dried morel mushrooms
- 1 qt kombu broth (see page 25 for recipe)
- 1 Tbsp soy sauce
- ¼ tsp salt
- 2 Tbsp vegetable oil
- 1 qt water

Instructions

❶ Soak the dried morel mushrooms in water to rehydrate. Wash the white radishes, peel them, and cut them into evenly-sized chunks. In a soup pot, add water and the white radish chunks. Boil for 10 minutes to remove any bitterness from the radishes, then remove them from the pot and set aside for later use.

❷ In the kombu broth, add the white radish chunks, rehydrated morel mushrooms, soy sauce, salt, and vegetable oil in turn. Transfer everything to a stewing pot and simmer for one hour.

Morel Mushroom Sweet Soup

This dish is a bold experiment in ingredient pairing for me. Morel mushrooms and coconut are commonly paired in soups, and the combination of sweetness and savory flavors blends together perfectly. This time, I had a sudden idea to add a few hawthorn berries, and unexpectedly, the sour-sweet taste made the dish even more appetizing.

Ingredients

- 1 coconut
- 2 dried morel mushrooms
- 4 hawthorn berries

Instructions

❶ Start by processing the coconut. Pour the coconut water into a stewing pot, then scoop out the coconut meat and cut it into small pieces before adding it to the pot.

❷ Soak the dried morel mushrooms in water for 1 hour to rehydrate, then add them to the pot. Stew over low heat for 15 minutes. After that, add the hawthorn berries and continue stewing over low heat for another 5 minutes.

Buckwheat Noodles with Salt and Pepper Oyster Mushroom

I still remember a few years ago, eating salt and pepper oyster mushrooms at a small food stall in Yunnan Province, China. They were crispy, flavorful, and had a delightful chewiness. After returning home, I tried to grow oyster mushrooms myself. I bought an oyster mushroom stick and placed it on the balcony, spraying some water on it. Within a few days, I was able to harvest a full basin of oyster mushrooms.

Ingredients

A

- 3 oz oyster mushrooms
- ¼ tsp cornstarch
- 1 c vegetable oil
- a pinch of salt
- ½ oz tricolor beans tempeh

B

- ¼ oz mung bean sprouts
- ¼ oz edamame
- ¼ oz crushed seaweed flakes with sesame
- 3 oz buckwheat noodles
- 1 Tbsp soy sauce
- 1 tsp brown rice vinegar
- ¼ oz pea tips (optional)

Instructions

❶ Use set A to make the salt and pepper mushrooms. After washing the oyster mushrooms, squeeze them dry. Sprinkle with salt and let them marinate for 5 minutes. Then coat them with cornstarch. In a small pot, heat the vegetable oil over low heat. Once the oil is hot, carefully add the cornstarch-coated mushrooms and fry until crispy and golden brown. Remove from the pot and place them on paper towels to absorb excess oil. The tricolor beans tempeh can also be fried in the oil until cooked through, then cut into small pieces.

❷ For set B, mix soy sauce and brown rice vinegar for seasoning in a serving bowl. Cook the buckwheat noodles, mung bean sprouts, and edamame in boiling water until cooked, then drain and add them to the bowl. Add the prepared salt and pepper mushrooms. Assemble all the ingredients and sprinkle with crushed seaweed flakes. When plating, decorate with pea tips or any other green vegetable that can be eaten raw if desired.

Plant-Based Bowl with Monkey Head Mushroom

The appearance of monkey head mushrooms is fuzzy, just like a little monkey's head, which is adorable. Every time I cook monkey head mushrooms, I can't help marveling at their soft and resilient texture. No matter what cooking method you use, they can absorb the essence of seasonings to the fullest, bringing a delightful surprise to the diners in terms of taste.

Ingredients

A

- 2 dried monkey head mushrooms
- 3 Tbsp low gluten flour
- 1 Tbsp soy sauce
- 2 tsp coconut sugar
- 1 tsp white sesame
- ½ c vegetable oil
- ⅕ c water

B

- 1 oz edamame kernels
- ¼ oz purple cabbage
- ¼ avocado
- ½ oz roasted seaweed flakes
- 3 oz brown rice

Instructions

❶ Use set A to make the sauced monkey head mushrooms. Soak the dried monkey head mushrooms in water for one hour. After soaking, wash them thoroughly with clean water 2 to 3 times, then soak them again for half an hour. Once softened, remove the roots. Boil the soaked monkey head mushrooms in boiling water for 3 to 5 minutes until cooked. Squeeze tightly to remove excess water, then tear them into pieces.

❷ Mix the low gluten flour and water to form a batter. Then dip the monkey head mushroom pieces into the batter and prepare them for frying. In a small pot, heat the vegetable oil over low heat. Once hot, carefully add the batter-coated monkey head mushrooms to the oil and fry until crispy and golden brown. Remove from the pot and place them on paper towels to absorb excess oil.

❸ Mix the soy sauce and coconut sugar until evenly mixed. In a frying pan, add the fried monkey head mushrooms. Stir-fry briefly, then add the sauce mixture. Stir-fry until the sauce thickens. Before serving, sprinkle some white sesame seeds as garnish.

❹ For set B, cook the edamame kernels in a pot of boiling water for about 10 minutes until tender. Wash the purple cabbage and slice it into thin shreds. Cut the avocado into chunks. Soak the brown rice for about 4 to 8 hours beforehand. Add water 1 cm above the level of the rice and boil it in a pot for approximately 20 minutes until done.

❺ Assemble all the ingredients and add roasted seaweed flakes.

Bell Pepper and Enoki Mushrooms with Tomato Sauce

Enoki mushrooms are fragrant and tender, with a deliciously smooth texture. This dish pairs enoki mushrooms with green bell peppers and tomato sauce. The slightly spicy fresh bell peppers is combined with the tomato sauce made from fresh tomatoes, giving the dish a tangy, spicy, and refreshing taste.

Ingredients

- 4 oz green bell peppers
- 4 oz enoki mushrooms
- 2 cherry tomatoes
- 1 large tomato
- 1 tsp tomato sauce
- 2 tsp soy sauce
- 2 Tbsp vegetable oil
- ¼ tsp salt

Instructions

❶ Wash the bell peppers and cut them into segments approximately 5 centimeters long, removing the seeds.

❷ After washing the enoki mushrooms, tear them apart and stuff them into the segments of bell peppers. Brush a layer of oil onto a frying pan, then fry the stuffed bell peppers with enoki mushrooms until cooked. At the same time, lightly fry the cherry tomatoes. Transfer everything to a plate and set aside.

❸ For the large tomato, pick one which is soft and tender for better juice extraction. After peeling the tomato, cut it into chunks. In a pan, add vegetable oil and heat it up. Then, add the tomato chunks and cook them. Next, add the tomato sauce, soy sauce, salt, and optionally a little water. Finally, add the fried bell peppers stuffed with enoki mushrooms and cook for about 1 minute. Once everything is cooked and the sauce has reduced, remove from the heat and serve.

Rose and White Fungus Sweet Soup

The history of consuming white fungus in China is long-standing. In ancient times, white fungus was considered a rare and precious wild fungus. Since they grew in deep mountain valleys and dense forests, it was difficult for people to pick them. Nowadays, you can easily buy ready-to-use dried white fungus or fresh white fungus in stores or online. This dish uses a stewing method, combining fresh white fungus and yellow rock sugar, preserving the original nutrients of the ingredients. This food has the effects of nourishing *yin*, moisturizing the lungs, nourishing the stomach, improving the production of body fluids, and moisturizing the skin. Adding the rose not only adds a floral fragrance but also enhances the beauty benefits.

Ingredients

- 1 oz fresh white fungus
- ¼ oz yellow rock sugar
- 1 dried rose
- 1 qt purified water

Instructions

❶ Wash the fresh white fungus thoroughly and tear it into small pieces.

❷ Add the washed white fungus pieces, yellow rock sugar, and purified water to the stew pot. Stew for 20 minutes.

❸ Add the dried rose before serving.

Appendix
Conversions

Volume	
US Standard	Metric (Approximate)
¼ tsp	1.25 ml
½ tsp	2.5 ml
1 tsp	5 ml
½ Tbsp	7.5 ml
1 Tbsp	15 ml
⅛ c	30 ml
¼ c	60 ml
⅓ c	80 ml
½ c	125 ml
1 c	250 ml
2 c (1 pt)	500 ml
1 qt	1 l

Temperature	
Fahrenheit	Celsius (Approximate)
250–275	130–140
300	150
325	165
350	175
375	190
400	200
425	220
450	230
475	245

Weight	
Avoirdupois	Metric (Approximate)
¼ oz	7 g
½ oz	15 g
1 oz	30 g
2 oz	60 g
3 oz	90 g
4 oz	115 g
5 oz	150 g
6 oz	175 g
7 oz	200 g
8 oz (½ lb)	225 g
9 oz	250 g
10 oz	300 g
11 oz	325 g
12 oz	350 g
13 oz	375 g
14 oz	400 g
15 oz	425 g
16 oz (1 lb)	450 g
1½ lb	750 g
2 lb	900 g
2¼ lb	1 kg
3 lb	1.4 kg
4 lb	1.8 kg